A Mildred L. Batchelder Honor Book
An ALA Notable Children's Book
An ALA Best Book for Young Adults
A Book Sense Children's Pick
A 2006 Sydney Taylor Notable Book
A Bank Street Best Children's Book of the Year

★ "The honest conflict about haunting issues in daily life is prime teen material, and readers on all sides of the war-peace continuum, here and there, will find much to talk about." —*Booklist*, starred review

"Recommended for its different perspective on life in contemporary Israel." —*Kirkus Reviews*

"A girl who thinks for herself, questions reality, and sees the poetry in life . . . Zenatti is a typical older youth in a situation that most American teens will never experience. . . . This book could generate discussions about the idea of national service, Israel, and the Middle East, and cultural similarities and differences among teens." —*VOYA*

"*When I Was a Soldier* is compelling—not because it tells an unconventional story, but because it tells a universal story which happens to be set in a troubled and misunderstood land." —Bookslut.com

"A unique coming-of-age tale that will appeal equally to adolescents and adults." —*World Jewish Digest*

When I Was a
SOLDIER

When I Was a

SOLDIER

a memoir by
Valérie Zenatti

translated by
Adriana Hunter

ïi institut français

This book is supported by the French Ministry for Foreign Affairs, as part of the
Burgess programme headed for the French Embassy in London by the
Institut Français du Royaume-Uni

Published by Bloomsbury U.S.A. Children's Books
175 Fifth Avenue, New York, NY 10010
Distributed to the trade by Holtzbrinck Publishers

The Library of Congress has cataloged the hardcover edition as follows:
Zenatti, Valérie.
[Quand j'étais soldate. French]
When I was a soldier : a memoir / by Valérie Zenatti ; translated by
Adriana Hunter.—1st U.S. ed.
p.   cm.
ISBN-13: 978-1-58234-978-7 • ISBN-10: 1-58234-978-9 (hardcover)
1. Zenatti, Valérie. 2. Women soldiers—Israel—Biography. 3. Jews, French—
Israel—Biography. 4. Israel—Armed Forces—Biography. I. Title.
U55.Z5A3 2005   956.9405'4'092   [B]   2004060888

_____

ISBN-13: 978-1-59990-059-9 • ISBN-10: 1-59990-059-9 (paperback)

Typeset by Dorchester Typesetting Group Ltd.
Printed in the U.S.A. by Quebecor World Fairfield
3 5 7 9 10 8 6 4 2

All papers used by Bloomsbury U.S.A. are natural, recyclable products made
from wood grown in well-managed forests. The manufacturing processes conform
to the environmental regulations of the country of origin.

My thanks to the Centre National du Livre for pacifying my bank manager while I was writing this book.

To Myriam, who is 'noudnikit' and wonderful.
To Geneviève, who understands.

We open our hearts the better to tell our secrets.

M.H.

PART ONE

THREE GIRLS
IN THE MIDDLE OF THE DESERT

'We're three losers in a land of losers,' Yulia says, spitting her words out and raising her eyebrows in an expression no one would dare argue with. 'This is the arsehole of the world,' she goes on, 'and nothing special ever came out of the arsehole of the world.'

I look into those big blue eyes she's so proud of, especially since she got her contacts. She used to have horrible plastic glasses, with really thick lenses, and she squinted. Long-sighted, astigmatic and with a twinkle in her eye, as my aunt would say. She carried the burden of it all through her child-hood. Since she swapped her glasses for two tiny lenses, it's as if she wants to make the whole world pay for her past humiliations. She's getting her revenge. Sometimes all you can see in her eyes is anger and contempt, or – worse than that – she's lying and her eyes are dressed up in this immea-surable innocence, all blue and transparent, as she talks to one of her teachers, or to a boy. I hate her big blue eyes. I hate my best friend's eyes with a sneaky, furious, impotent sort of hate. And I feel just as much loathing for the way she sometimes speaks, deliberately foul-mouthed and hard, as if she's saying, 'I'm free now. I'm no longer my parents' nice little girl.'

She's my best friend, all the same . . . I have to admit it and she seems to agree. At school we've been classified as inseparable, no one could imagine bumping into one of us without the other. We've been sitting next to each other systematically for four years, and we phone each other on average eight times a day. When I'm not with her I'm with Rahel, my other best friend.

They were both born in what was once the USSR. Yulia's from Tashkent in Uzbekistan. She likes saying those names in front of me – Tashkent, Samarkand – as if there were treasure sparkling on every street corner back there. In front of other people from Russia she emphasises the fact that her father's of German origin and her mother Romanian; I can tell she's ashamed of Uzbekistan. Everyone else seems to think that that's where the arsehole of the world is. Personally, I haven't got very fixed ideas about the anatomy of our planet.

Rahel was born in Benderi, a little town near Kishinev in Moldova. When she pronounces the name of her childhood town, she stresses the second 'e' and gives the 'r' a liquid rolling sound as they do in Slavic languages, and she lingers on the 'i' with an affectionate smile. She is definitely what they call homesick.

I was born in Nice, in France, and that's very unusual. Remarkable, even. That's what makes me seem a bit different to everyone, and what makes me interesting – or even charming – to some. I only have to open my mouth for people to gather round. It makes it easier to get to know people but it can be exasperating, especially when you just have to 'say something in French'. *Baudelaire, Camembert, solitude, enfant terrible* . . . whatever comes into my head. What matters to them is the sound of it. Especially words which contain e, u, an, in, on (*de, du, dans, dindon*), all sounds that don't exist in their language and which they find so beguiling and exotic. It's thanks to them that I realised a language is first and foremost a kind of music, an assembly of sounds. I say absolutely anything to them, because I can't think what to say to people who don't understand a word I'm saying, and they love it. It breaks my heart, because I really like words: I'm fascinated by them, I respect them, I try to penetrate their mysterious depths, and to use them advisedly in both languages: my mother tongue, French, and the foreign one, Hebrew.

But everyone else couldn't care less, and never stop saying, 'Oh please, say something in French!'

We live in Beersheva, a town of 100,000 inhabitants in the Negev Desert in Israel. Seen from the sky, it looks like Atlanta (minus the CNN building and the Olympic stadium): grey cubes plonked on the grey sand. Anyone who thinks that a desert is always an expanse of fine white sand, with a leafy little oasis here and there, has watched too many cartoons. Lucky things, I envy them!

Ever since I arrived here five years ago with my parents and my sister, I've thought the desert was ugly, unsettling and pointless. Only the sun, which disappears every evening in a magnificent blaze, justifies the fact that there's nothing else there.

I have two Russian best friends. They have blue eyes and chestnut-brown hair but they don't look alike at all. We have turned, are turning or are about to turn eighteen. In two months' time we'll be sweating it out over the trials of the *baccalauréat*.

In six months, at the latest, we'll be changing out of our jeans and T-shirts into khaki shirts and trousers.

The army for all of us. Soldier girls. Yulia, Rahel and myself.

At the moment we're lying on the lawn in the middle of the horseshoe shape created by the apartment buildings where we live. The estate is called a 'residential area for new immigrants'; there are no signs telling you to keep off the grass, and people speak in about fifteen different languages.

We're talking about the night before, going over it again and again: a party organised at Ilan's house – he's one of a group of boys who come about as close to normality as we're going to get.

'The same old story! It's always the same old story!' Yulia groans. 'Some Coke, some vodka, the boys dancing like drunken ducks, the girls getting depressed: you sweat, your make-up runs, you go to the toilet to put another layer on, but who for? Who for?'

Rahel and I make the prudent decision to remain silent confronted with such despair. We're quite used to Yulia's whining. In a couple of minutes she'll get up and cut us dead with one sharp sentence, us and this whole rotten hell-hole . . . or she might change to a new subject: herself, for example.

Which of course she does this time.

'Anyway, as usual, they all looked at me all night . . . I sometimes wonder why . . . It's not as if I was as well dressed as you, Val.'

I steal a quick glance at Rahel who's making no effort to hide a knowing smile.

'Yes,' Rahel agrees, 'they were all at your feet, rapt, miserable, devoted, drooling . . . It was too touching for words . . . Who did you decide on?'

A furious stare from Yulia.

A feeling of dismay bears down on me.

If it goes on like this, there's going to be a row, screaming, insults thrown back and forth. And I'm terrified of anger. I go pale, I go red, I start to shake as soon as people raise their voices. Standing there silently with my eyes beginning to prickle, I feel stupid and redundant. Quickly, change the subject. On to the *bac*, for example.

'Have you done your notes for *Crime and Punishment*?'

'Yes,' replies Rahel, 'but I'm having trouble with it. In Russian, it's about crime, but in Hebrew it's been translated as "sin". It's not the same at all. Raskolnikov commits a crime, full stop.'

'But the crime was a sin,' I counter. 'Dostoyevsky must

have seen it like that, he was very much a believer.'

'What about *L'Etranger*?' Yulia intervenes. 'Have you finished it?'

'No problem. I've read it three times, I've done all my notes on Camus, Algeria, the absurd, the death penalty . . . Let's just hope the question comes up!'

'It's hardly surprising you're so crazy about him, he's French!'

'So what? That's got nothing to do with it. Are you crazy about Dostoyevsky just because he's Russian?'

'No,' says Yulia.

'Yes,' Rahel contradicts her.

'Will you lend me your notes on Camille?' Yulia asks me casually.

'Try and pronounce his name properly for once. "Camille" is a girl's name! This is Camus. Ca-mus! U! But, umm . . . about the notes . . . sorry, but there's no point. I've written them all in French.'

I'm sure she's seen through my hesitation from the way she turns her head sharply. But there's a little smile spreading over her lips as she tilts her chin forward.

'Hey, girls, look who's coming.'

We follow her gaze. Ilana, alias Paint-pot, is coming towards us. Along with boys, teachers, subjects for the *bac* and the army, she's in our top five favourite topics of conversation. We could talk about her outfits for hours. She regularly commits two mistakes which we rate as unforgivable: she wears red with pink, and her lipstick unfailingly smudges on to her teeth. We make fun of her pretty much openly. I know it's nasty, but we need Ilana: she's the sort of girl that absolutely anyone can stand next to and feel luminous, beautiful and chic. Anyway, she's clearly very interested in our conversations, even when she hasn't been invited to join in. Her ears drag along the ground and her suspicious expression reminds me of a nosey old spinster running a pre-war boarding house – not that I've ever met one of course, but imagination is one of mankind's distinguishing features. The girl would make an excellent spy.

'Hi! Have you heard the latest?'

'No!' we chorus in reply.

That's an eternal truth. No one has ever heard the latest news. Except, of course, whoever is triumphantly announcing it.

'Orange is THE colour for the summer. Can you believe that?'

'Yuk!'

'No way!'

'It can't be!'

For no particular reason, we decreed one fine day that the colour orange was beneath us. Only suitable for girls with no future. Ilana knows this and she's taking pleasure in giving our little group a good dig.

'Mind you,' I pipe up, 'I couldn't care less about orange. You see, I'm going to be in khaki long before you.'

A respectful silence ensues.

'Right, I'm off,' I say, jumping up. 'I've got work in an hour.'

And I walk off over the lawn, taking big strides, trying to

look as much like Faye Dunaway in *Bonnie and Clyde* as I can. I don't look back, but I know the girls are watching me. If there's one thing I'm sure of it's that they envy me my legs. That's one good reason not to despair of this life.

At school, lessons end at 2 p.m. There isn't a canteen or a lunch break – we study in one long stretch then we're free for the rest of the day, to revise, play sport or watch TV. I work in a big chemist, a chain, where I'm employed under the pompous title of 'display coordinator'. Basically, this means that I have to go up and down the aisles lining products up so that the shelves look full to bursting, with all the shampoos, deodorants and sanitary towels right up against each other. Apparently it makes the customers want to break up this perfect order, and therefore to buy. From time to time I'm requisitioned by the perfume department for gift-wrapping, and I keep myself entertained inventing really sophisticated wrapping techniques with three or five folds in the paper and with two or four turned-back edges. I'm paid to spend time doing something beautifully when someone else is going to undo it with one swift movement.

When Rafi, the boss, took me on he detailed Extrapharm's philosophy to me for twenty minutes: the customer is king, whatever they want is an order, we are slaves at their service, and when they drive us headlong towards a nervous breakdown while they hesitate between washing powder with or without fabric conditioner (terrified that their wives will create a scene if they don't buy what they were told to), we have to flash them a sweet amiable smile, and soothe their fears as we guide them through this critical decision.

After giving me two or three examples of situations I might well come across in my new and wonderful career with such a promising future, Rafi handed me the charter for Extrapharm employees, which reminds them that they must grovel willingly before customers. I very quickly learned it by heart, not out of fanaticism or servility, but because it was posted up on the walls of the toilets and the cloakroom, where I spend a certain amount of time every day. Extract:

Do not say: *This isn't my department, ask X in department Z*, but: *Follow me, I will take you to someone familiar with that department.*

Do not say: *We don't have any more in stock*, but: *That product has been very popular, and we're waiting for a delivery any day now. If you leave me your details I would be delighted to let you know as soon as it has arrived.*

Do not say: *Goodbye*, but: *Thank you for being a regular customer. I hope we'll see you again soon.*

Obviously the seven other commandments are in the same vein.

At first I couldn't help biting my lip when I saw the expression of bemusement on the faces of little old men and women from Poland or Morocco, left speechless by such a show of courtesy, but then I got used to it. I sort of put myself on autopilot, and if I ever forget the profoundly *relational* nature of my work, my watch is there to remind me. You see, the last article on the charter instructs us to:

Put your watch on your right wrist, not your left, so that every time you check the time you will be reminded that you are an exceptional employee, in an exceptional organisation, serving exceptional customers.

If you ask me, the shrewd directors of Extrapharm chose the watch as a mnemonic device because they must have realised that checking their watches was the most frequently made gesture amongst their employees. The charter doesn't specify whether the organisation would buy watches for employees who don't have them.

Let me also make it clear that I'm underpaid – a pitiful hourly rate which adds up to precious little for my 120 hours' work a month, after deductions for social security and for my pension contribution (although I have trouble appreciating the usefulness of the latter). Being an exceptional employee in an exceptional organisation is pretty good in itself; you can't go asking for too much money on top of that.

When I think about it, I'm convinced that later in life I'll be a trade unionist. Or perhaps a revolutionary. And the day I am, they'll be adding two noughts on all the pay slips or, even better, there won't be any pay slips at all, and money won't be this weird thing I'm prepared to act the fool for (with some talent, apparently) in those aisles which smell of a mixture of soap, washing powder and expensive perfume. The day I am, no one will feel humiliated any longer just for being poor, and no organisation will be run like a mini dictatorship.

I'm dreaming.

I know I am, but then that's my default setting. In a

moment of pompous excess (I sometimes get them), I once actually wrote: 'I'm not sure I live, but I'm quite sure I dream.'

(Dream: 1. A series of thoughts, images and sensations occurring in a person's mind during sleep. 2. An unrealistic or self-deluding fantasy.)

In my own personal dictionary I would add: endless discussion with girlfriends, impassioned speculation about the future, formulating ideas about the 'real' life out there waiting for us. This comes with agonising decisions into the bargain: what will we do after the army? A six-month or year-long trip to Latin America or India, like so many other people, to clear our heads? Or studying first, and the grand tour afterwards? Yes, but if we meet a man, the ideal man, while we're sitting our *bac*, do we have to wave goodbye for ever to that trip of a lifetime, to that therapeutic freedom we dream about, somewhere far away, on a continent where there's nothing to remind us of the things we know? And what will we study? International relations? History? Communication studies? To become what? Diplomats? Journalists? Press officers? What sort of life are we going to have? The future's so hazy, so unspecified, and we would so like it to be completely, completely different from what we're living now! Oh, for a wave of a wand to make it exciting and amazing and beautiful enough to make the whole world jealous. The future, at least for Rahel, Yulia and myself, is strangely like the word revenge.

I'm thinking about all this as I cycle over to Extrapharm. Thinking about my two friends who are so different, but who

23

are so important to me in equal measures. Thinking that I really deserve the holiday at Eilat on the Red Sea that we're planning to have straight after sitting the *bac* (when my hands are black with dust by the end of this evening, that will be proof that I've earned another instalment, half a night in a youth hostel – I'll have to wait until tomorrow for the other half). Thinking that our stint in the army is like a long digression, a sub-clause in our lives, and we know nothing about what's in it. Thinking that I go to so much trouble to keep myself thinking like this – all the time, so busily, in a great endless whirl, always thinking about tomorrow – to make absolutely sure that I don't think about the fact that Jean-David went to live in Jerusalem a week ago already, and he hasn't rung me since.

AND NOW FOR
THE *BAC*

'Valeriiiiiiiiie!'

Six times a week, Yulia bellows my name as she passes beneath my window on her way to school.

'I'll be right down!'

That's a bit of a lie. Right down means at least five minutes. Half the contents of my wardrobe is strewn over the bed, and I'm still not dressed. What to wear? What to choose? Maybe green? Someone once told me that it brought good luck. But I've only got one green jacket, and it's dirty . . . What was Yulia wearing again? I hardly saw her. Jeans and a blue T-shirt, I think, unless it was white trousers and a pink T-shirt. I wander up and down, fiddle nervously with clothes without actually looking at them.

Indecision. Panic.

First *bac* exams today: history this morning, Bible studies this afternoon. To be honest, at the moment, I'm not even thinking about them.

I just don't know what to wear.

I quickly snatch a white skirt from its hanger with one hand as I demolish the pile of T-shirts with the other to get the bottom one, the black one. Black and white. Two extremes. All or nothing. 'Be the best or the worst, but never be just average' Gidi once told us – he's our history teacher and half the girls in school have been or still are in love with him (the other half having decided not to explore the question but to have real love affairs). Black and white, then. On top of the advantage of expressing a particular philosophy, they're two colours which incontrovertibly stave off any errors of taste.

The intercom pierces my eardrums. Yulia's getting impatient, and I don't blame her: it's a quarter to eight. I scoot past Mum, who's got her anxious face on.

'You haven't eaten anything . . .'

'Don't worry. I've got loads of cereal bars in my bag.'

'Will you come back at lunchtime, then? I'll make some –'

A second ring, more threatening than the first.

'No, we're going to eat at Rahel's, her parents aren't there.'

She's disappointed. Really hurt, even. If I leave like this, having upset her, I'm going to fail the lot, obviously.

So I quickly say, 'Make something fantastic for this evening. I'll be here.'

She smiles instantly and says, 'BREAK A LEG.' Then she whispers in my ear, 'I know you'll pass, anyway. It's just a formality for you.'

One day I'll have to look up why 'break a leg' is meant to bring you luck. There must be some logic to it but I can't quite see it at the moment. I could also do with understanding why my mother has such faith in me, when I constantly have doubts about myself. But I definitely won't find the answer to that in any reference book.

Yulia's sitting on the wall drumming a rapid little rhythm with her long hard nails.

'You took ages! You've decided to give up all idea of the *bac* and make a career as a cashier at Extrapharm, is that it?'

'No. I didn't know what to wear.'

'Well, you found something! And, actually, that skirt's not bad. Anyway, what does it matter. I should remind you these are *written* exams, not *oral* ones.'

'I know. But I wanted to feel good – pretty, even. Just for the sake of it. For me.'

'Yeah, right.' (She couldn't care less.) 'So, then, how *are* you feeling?'

'Weird . . .'

'Apart from that?'

'Odd. Empty. Like an alien. Well, you know . . .'

'No, I don't.'

'Come on! This is just an exam like any other. After all, they're not expecting us to know more than at any other time in the year. But at the same time, everyone makes such a meal of it. Ever since I moved into the first year I've been given an earful of the *bac*: "You start working towards your *bac* right now," our English teacher used to say. "You'll see, when you sit your *bac* . . ." all the others used to say. I really thought it was a question of life and death. That anyone who recovered from it was superhuman. This morning it feels like it's not me who's going to school with you. It's like I'm watching myself doing things, without actually being involved.'

'Basically, it's because you're thinking about Jean-David.'

She missed an opportunity to keep her mouth shut. She could have given me a right-hook smack on my jaw bone and it would have felt like a gentle caress in comparison. We walk through the school gate.

Rahel is already there. She comes over towards us, eyes sparkling and slightly out of breath. That's how you know when she's worried or upset. She always refuses to express any emotion in words. When Liron, her first boyfriend, told her he loved her for the first time, she told him, 'It's not serious, you'll get over it.' He never re-offended and they split up shortly after that. Mind you, he should have been able to understand her, he's strange enough himself.

'It's a pain,' she told us. 'There are six exam rooms, and it's done alphabetically.'

Her surname starts with a B, Yulia's with a K, and mine with a Z. Between the three of us we cover the whole alphabet. There are times when I think we represent the world in all its diversity.

The bell rings. We kiss to wish each other good luck, and everyone watches us. It's very French that, kissing friends. Yulia loves the habit, having watched some old Sophie Marceau film too many times (and secretly identified with her).

The herds of students make their way to the exam rooms. There are those who are still revising, checking dates, asking for tips from the school brains. And these brains, who are often girls, look horrified and start shrieking, 'I've forgotten everything! I've forgotten everything!' in shrill, disjointed voices. Others seem very detached, there are couples with their arms round each other, as if they're beyond the whole thing, as if the fact of displaying their love in front of everyone is in itself a passport to adulthood. In Hebrew (and in German too, I think), the *bac* is actually called 'Maturity'.

The history exam (which counts for three marks) is divided into two parts:

1. History of the Holocaust (1 mark);
2. General History (2 marks).

That's how it is. The Holocaust is separate. It's a history subject within and yet outside the history exam. A compulsory section, almost a whole subject in itself. It's not a question which might just happen to crop up, like the Dreyfus affair, Napoleonic Europe, the golden age of the Spanish Jews or the Crusades. There isn't a single Israeli who can sit the *bac* without being questioned on the Holocaust. Six million dead, explain when, who, where, how, why. Come to grips with the statistics, the dates, the torturers' names; learn by heart passages from *Mein Kampf* and Nazi propaganda slogans; know the list of camps, in the order in which they were established; distinguish between work camps and death camps; know that there was a whole life and culture in the ghettos – schools, theatre productions, operas. Remember the complicated spelling of the words Einsatzgruppen and

Obersturmbannführer; don't forget the selection process, those on the right who would be gassed immediately, and those on the left who would live a little, dying off every day. Conscientiously learn the Nuremberg Laws, that's where the extermination starts. People are singled out, set apart, pointed at – that's already killing them slightly. The Final Solution, the Wannsee conference, read everything you can on those subjects, make notes, revision cards. It's such a huge story, with so many thousands of books, chapters and sub-chapters, the story of the extermination of European Jews: Germany, France, the Netherlands, Belgium, Poland, Russia, Czechoslovakia and Yugoslavia (as they were then), Greece, Hungary, Italy; God, Europe seems a big place!

So the exam on the Holocaust starts the five days of exams, and is the first step on the road to 'Maturity'.

I sit down and, like everyone else, I put a bottle of water in front of me. It's amazing how much you can drink during an exam. The papers are about to be handed out and the hubbub gradually dies down. Now we only communicate in signs: Alon and Miki blow up their cheeks and roll their eyes to show that it's not going to be a piece of cake; Tal and Rafi pull silly faces, taking some of the tension out of the moment; the boys seem more wound up than the girls, some have laid bets on which questions will come up. It's two minutes to eight. The deputy head comes in holding a large brown plastic envelope at arm's length. She turns it in every direction to prove that it's completely sealed, then she takes the papers out as if they are the most valuable things she has held in her hands for years.

The instructions, which we'll come to know by heart over the next few days, are given out by a geek who's almost lost his voice: Avi, a maths student.

'The exam starts at eight o'clock precisely and will end at ten o'clock precisely. We will then proceed to collect your papers and to hand out the General History papers. That exam will last three hours. The use of calculators is strictly prohibited . . .'

Surname, first name:
Identity number:
Date of birth:

' . . . as is the use of any form of dictionary . . .'

School: Date of exam:
Exam: Mark:

'If you need to use the toilet, you should be accompanied. No more than one pupil may leave the room at any one time. You may not leave the exam room for more than five minutes . . .'

History of the Holocaust. 1 mark.

'May I remind you that you have a choice of two questions. Don't forget to indicate which question you have chosen. May I also remind you that you should not under any circumstances, and I stress not under any circumstances, put your name on to the exam papers, or anything that might make it possible for the examiner to identify you . . .'

Question number one: 1935–1938: *Describe and comment, with emphasis on the salient events in these four years, on the implementation of the Nazi policy of persecution with respect to German Jews.*

Question number two: *The Warsaw ghetto, 1940–1943.*

There are a few stifled whoops of joy around the room. Clearly, some people have won their bets. I hesitate a bit between the two questions. The first is relatively technical, 'solid': you just have to refer to the Nuremberg Laws and the Kristallnacht, to analyse the development of social violence encouraged by the law, then the onset of physical violence, the destruction of possessions and ultimately of whole lives. The second question is much wider. The ghetto is life and death side by side, families crammed together, forced labour, famine, illness, the songs, the culture, the round-ups, humiliations, separations and the eventual revolt led by a handful of young people our age. Sixteen, seventeen, eighteen years old, with a gun in their hands, a gun and a few bullets to stand up to the Wehrmacht for more than a month; a gun, some grenades and a few bullets, against tanks and even planes. Doing anything to die with their heads held high, as fighters, as soldiers facing other soldiers and not as victims facing their oppressors. I'm no longer in an exam room, I'm no longer sitting my *bac*. I'm standing in front of one of the leaders of that revolt in the Warsaw ghetto, Mordehaï Anilevitch, whose picture I've seen at the Yad Vashem museum. A slightly hazy, black and white picture of a handsome and resolute young man; of course he was very handsome and very resolute. And soon I too will have a weapon in my hands, I too will be a soldier, but there's no comparison and the parallel I've just drawn strikes me as ridiculous.

I'm letting my mind wander and the time's tick, tick, ticking by. I can tell that if I choose the ghetto I'm going to write some lyrical piece, I'm going to put down these sad, impassioned sentences, I might even cry as I write. The tears will make splodges on my work and I'll automatically lose ten points (we're marked out of a hundred, and, according to the teachers, presentation must be worth a good ten points).

It'll have to be the first question, then.

The maths geek is counting flies. Every now and then he walks up and down the rows, looking important. Every quarter of an hour he announces how much time we have left. He looks sad. Maybe he's waiting too, waiting for a phone call that never comes. Or worse still: he's never been in love and maths is his only refuge.

In the space of three years, the Nazi regime establishes an apparatus of violence within the framework of the law. The machinery of hatred, which leads from exclusion within society to the destruction of possessions and of lives themselves, is set in motion. A regime of terror is being established in Germany, under the very eyes of other European countries. The darkest page of human history is being written.

My wrist is hurting but overall I'm pleased with myself. I've written eight pages and I think they're quite clear. I finally look up for the first time in two hours. Those who have finished are catching each other's eyes. Ilana and Rinat, the two stuck-up cows, are breathing heavily as they cover their papers with hasty sentences right up to the last minutes, and then beg the maths nerd to let them finish. Just one more word . . . just another quarter of a point, perhaps . . .

We don't have time to catch our breath. We're already having to turn our attention to the General History paper, re-writing our names, the subject, the date . . . There are three questions on offer:

1. The Birth of Nations;
2. The American Civil War;
3. The October Revolution.

I don't hesitate for a moment, and I start to write, before I've even thought about it, on the third subject. I start like this:

The reign of Tsar Alexander II gave rise to a great feeling of hope in Russia. He was preparing to give his country a first Constitution when he was assassinated in Paris in 1881. Alexander III, far from pursuing this evolution towards democracy, subjected the mujiks to further constraints. Anger and frustration began to germinate . . .

I went back a long way, I'm aware of that. The October Revolution was in 1917, not in 1881! A grumpy examiner could even strike out the whole first paragraph with a line of blood-red ink – not that I'll ever see it but it'll make him feel better. It's just . . . I can't help myself: I'm a fan of Alexander

II, I talk about him at every opportunity. It must be thanks to a gorgeous film I saw about him and his mistress Katia. I've devoured everything I could find to read about them. They say it was Katia who persuaded the Tsar to adopt more liberal policies, that she was his inspiration. When it suits me I do like to believe those sort of rumours (even when they've been seriously romanticised). Alexander II apparently also wanted to have her crowned as Empress after his wife died (and she was described in my books as a colourless old woman, thin as a rake with stern features, in other words the exact opposite of this gentle mistress). He didn't have time, and Katia – whose full name was Katarina Dolgorouki – was unceremoniously driven out by the new incumbent. She went into exile in France, and died in Nice.

So basically just mentioning Alexander II puts me in a good mood and at the end of this first morning of exams I'm feeling confident.

In the break I meet up with Rahel and Yulia. The first prostrate, the second on edge. I don't dare ask any questions. Yulia puts her arm round Rahel and I do the same, without a word. We stay like that for several minutes, rocking her gently, driving away curious onlookers clustering round us as if there's been an accident.

'Do you want to grab a sandwich or should we go and eat at your house like we planned?' I whisper.

She stares stubbornly at the ground then looks up sharply and, with a note of false cheerfulness which I find painful, she trills, 'We're going back to my house, of course! My mum's filled the whole fridge and made me promise we'd raid it.'

'Let's race there.'

'OK!'

That's something we do. It's peculiar to the two of us. The minute there's something wrong with one of us, the other suggests a race. It's not to do with who's going to win. That's always Rahel, who holds the school record for 100m and 400m (regardless of the distance, she beats the boys, and we're incredibly proud of that). What matters is the feeling that we're so closely connected by running together. We throw off anything that's upsetting us, anything that's bothering us. Just another way of escaping from ourselves.

It's not much more than a hundred metres to the building where Rahel lives. We wait for Yulia, who's sauntering nonchalantly, her face tinged with superiority as well as incomprehension. I can hear the word 'childish' booming in her head. When she has that look on her face it's as if our friendship's being blown away. I've felt it for a few months now, and I know it for sure today. I force myself to think about something else, to try and guess what questions will come up in the Bible studies exam this afternoon.

'I completely panicked in General History,' Rahel whispers. 'And I didn't write a thing, absolutely nothing, apart from my name and the other details.'

I squeeze her hand really hard. I know she won't tell anyone what she's just confided in me. She's proud, she's secretive, she's complicated – some would even say twisted – but I love her like a sister, like my own double, like a friend I really would swear loyalty to for life, to death.

The whirlwind of exams starts again very soon, and the litany of instructions makes me feel as if I'm acting out the same scene again and again for the sadistic pleasure of a mysterious spectator.

Bible studies: the universalism of the prophet Amos's message.

Biology: the mechanism of DNA.

English: Martin Luther King's *I have a dream* speech.

Literature: the anti-hero in Dostoyevsky.

It was just after the literature exam that Jean-David had the very bad idea of ringing me. Stammering, contrite, embarrassed, he explained with endless sidetracking and convolutions that he'd met a girl in Jerusalem and that things were going pretty well between them. He was very sorry, but I was going off to the army anyway, so we weren't going to be able to see each other regularly, I'd be meeting other people, starting a new life . . . Obviously, we could still be friends, he'd love to see me again. I answered with a long silence before saying goodbye to him, in one breath, with the beginnings of a sob, then I ran to cry in Rahel and Yulia's arms, for a long time.

For the maths exam, which was the following day, I was dressed like God knows what. And I may not have shed any tears as I wrote about the Holocaust, but when it came to the trigonometry problems, which I can never completely resolve, they were covered in little splodges.

I will pass the *bac*, though, that's as good as definite. But it doesn't bother me either way, not right now. I'm just a walking wound. When the results come in October I'll be a soldier, I'll be living in that strange world where you go in as an adolescent and, apparently, come out as an adult.

COUNTDOWN TO THE ARMY

Last summer when I told my cousins in France that I'd be going into the army after my *bac*, they were completely gob-smacked. Especially the girls, who just couldn't understand what sort of reality might lie behind my words. Girls in the army, uniform, weapons and everything else seemed to be part of some mysterious folklore, like a game in which girls dress up as boys for a while. I could tell that they just could-n't understand at all, and I abandoned any idea of explaining it to them.

Here, the army is part of our lives. Long before we're actually enlisted, long before we're even called for the first medical check-up (the one that makes all the girls twitter with terror because they know that, in groups of five, they have to file naked past the doctors, who are mostly men, and the idea terrifies them).

Soldiers – boys and girls – are the heroes of the past, the

ones who won the war of independence, the Six Days' War and the Yom Kippur War. Every year on our Remembrance Day we're shown films and black and white photographs of soldiers so handsome they take your breath away looking into the camera and flashing tired, dazzling smiles at us. We come across them every day in the street, at the cinema, at the supermarket, clubbing, at the bus station; our neighbours' sons and daughters, our friends who were doing their *bac* the year before, in their khaki uniforms and, less frequently, in the grey air force uniform. They're on their way home from their bases, or on their way back there, they're relaxing, going out, flirting. No one notices them particularly, because there are too many of them, because it's normal and everyone's either been in, is in or will one day be in the army. But when a soldier falls asleep on someone's shoulder in the bus, all the passengers exchange these adoring looks and, in spite of themselves, the person who's acting as a cushion is very careful not to move, not to wake this eighteen-year-old boy or girl who's giving two or three of the best years of their life to their country, as they say. Because, where the army is concerned, everyone's agreed on one thing: it's very tiring, but it's essential.

The army and soldiers are always there – in the few films that are made in Israel, and in the countless songs that are played on a loop on the radio. Every album by Shlomo Artzi, my favourite Israeli singer, has at least one song about a soldier. The album that came out just before I joined the army, *July–August Heat*, felt like my own story, written specially for me, as if those summer months – the last two before the army – were really my own, summed up in fifteen songs: love petering out in pain and guilt, an aching feeling of nostalgia, and the darkness of this Intifada hanging over everything, consuming us and, some would say, threatening to devour our very souls.

Actually, last but not least, to the boys the army means girls and to the girls it means boys. In other words, every girl (let's just take them as the example) is hoping that in that vast catalogue of boys of eighteen to twenty-one she'll find the one she's waiting for and who certainly seems to be taking his time turning up, the one who'll mean something like this to her: 'I'm a man, a real man, strong but sensitive, I'm here to protect you.' And the others, the ones who already have a boyfriend, live in fear: they have nightmares every night that some ravishing soldier girl, some bombshell to die for in khaki, will bump into their boyfriend so far away and offer them a shoulder to cry on. Among other things, the army is our very own *commedia dell'arte*.

We're a nation of lunatics stranded between songs, the sea and war. A country in which death is conceivable from as early as eighteen, but this eventuality doesn't make anyone any more intelligent. A country where we're convinced that love lies waiting in those army bases surrounded by barbed wire, under a canvas tent, in a thick sleeping bag. This is my country, so I know and I understand all this almost physically. And yet I feel like a stranger to it, a foreigner.

I'd had plenty of time, months, to think about my last day before the fateful date. I would go to the swimming pool with

41

Jean-David, I would play tennis with him, I'd win of course, let's say 6–4, 6–4, 7–5, and he'd kiss me and whisper, 'Congratulations, Colonel', then we'd go back to my house where the whole group would join us, Yulia, Rahel and her boyfriend Freddy, Ilan, Rafi, Tova . . . Ilan would bring his guitar, they would all sing Russian songs that I don't understand but I love, Jean-David and I would parry with French songs and my mother would smile, with tears in her eyes, as she took pictures of us, saying, 'Oh, you gorgeous young things!' Jean-David would spend the night with me (I'd have spent days begging Mum to grant me this favour), and the following morning, on the 19th of September, he would go to the recruiting office with me, we'd hug and kiss for a long time with my friends watching tenderly, and the forty girls from Beersheva enrolling on the same day as me would be torn between jealousy and admiration, seeing me leaving such a cute boyfriend with his fair skin, his grunge-look jacket and his Marlboro reds.

It's the 18th of September and nothing's going according to plan. The main character in the whole script is cruelly absent from the roll-call and since this morning I've been muttering, 'Bastard, bastard, bastard.' It doesn't even hurt any more (as it has done all through the summer, which I've spent red-eyed listening to our favourite songs end to end) – now I'm just angry with him for spoiling my scenario.

This morning I went to work at Extrapharm for the last time. They all made a fuss of me and they even hung balloons for me in the stockroom with a banner: 'Soldier girl, go in peace and bring us back peace.' I found it all ridiculous and touching. They also gave me some Nina Ricci body milk. I thanked them warmly even though I knew that, with their employees' 30% reduction, it can't have cost them very much. I would have preferred the perfume and I'm furious no one thought of that. I'm in a filthy mood, I've got these grinding sounds in my head but here I am smiling, kissing people, laughing at the cheap jokes about the army that I've heard a hundred times, and eagerly accepting the things they keep telling me:

'You'll see, you'll grow up . . . the army changes everything . . . you'll be homesick . . . Not to mention your mother's cooking! It's for the country, it's a good thing, you have to do something for your country . . . It's an experience, the university of life . . .' I'm restraining myself. Containing myself. My replies are vague onomatopoeic grunts that no one listens to because I'm not there to talk, I'm there to listen to the well-meaning wisdom of these people proud of their own experiences, glad to have an opportunity to trot out their military memories for the umpteenth time, with the inevitable 'of course, it was harder in those days' on all their lips. They're kind, they've given me a present, they've even bought two bars of white chocolate (again with the 30% reduction), they've hardly let me do any work – 'with what you've got in store tomorrow you need to save yourself' – but I feel like sending them packing to Gaza (as we say round here), I feel like telling them to fuck off with their words which mean nothing to me, which don't get to me, I feel more and more grumpy, unhappy and angry, without really knowing why. I claim I have a headache so that I can leave early and no one questions me. And actually it's not a lie: the dull pain that I know so well when I get tense is already reverberating round my head. I take off my blue overall for the last time. I clock out. It's 3.27.

I go to the toilet and can't help seeing the famous charter with its ten commandments. I've got a big red marker pen in my bag. I take it out, it becomes very warm in my hand – or is it my hand which feels warm touching it? I've already forgotten the physics or chemistry lesson which would have cleared that up for me. I screw and unscrew the lid. I hesitate but it's not for fear of being caught. It's because I haven't actually thought about what I could write. I need one word, one punchy sentence to say it all, something definitive to express my feelings of revolt. An aphorism, something concise, a coined word, a stroke of genius. I finally opt for: 'And God said: "let there be rampant capitalism", and there was Extrapharm.' And I cited the reference: Genesis of exploited employees, chapter 1, verse 7.

I throw a quick goodbye to the assembled company and hop on my bike. I couldn't care less if they catch me – in fact it would be a good laugh to see their faces as the ten of them bundle into the toilet to comment on my thankless attitude – but I have to get home quickly. My head's exploding.

The apartment is empty. I take three aspirin. My things are laid out on my bed, carefully organised by Mum following the list sent to me by the army. Underwear has to be white, socks black or white, and it specifies 'without lace, coloured edging, patterns or other ornamentation'. Jewellery is completely forbidden during lessons. I have to have two weeks' worth of stuff. I know that I'm leaving tomorrow. I don't know when I'll get my first leave.

I look at the little piles with their perfect right angles, the brand new little wash-bag, bought for the occasion. It's almost as if I'm going to a holiday camp. Or on a trek. But who's ever been to holiday camp for two years? I suddenly feel a wave of panic. What about writing my will? This might be the time. This time tomorrow I'll be so far away . . . I add my personal stereo to the waiting clothes, and my favourite music, including some French music to have a little bit of France with me. And a book, something good that makes me want to laugh and to cry. Now that's my definition of a good book, a combination of happiness and despair.

Will I have time to read? It doesn't matter. You always have to have a book with you. And a notebook to write in. It's essential for survival.

The phone rings. I hesitate for a moment. It could be the manager from Extrapharm ringing to tell me how disappointed he is by my ungrateful attitude. After everything he's done for me . . . Leaving like that, defacing the ten commandments! I don't feel like listening to him. I don't feel like explaining myself. And the phone goes on ringing. We don't have an answerphone, they're too expensive. Never mind. I won't know whether it was him or someone else.

I wait for the ringing to stop before picking up the handset. I have to speak to someone, to dispel my nerves. Liouba, Yulia's little sister, tells me Yulia's gone into town, perhaps with Rahel, she's not really sure. Rahel's mother tells me her daughter's gone out, perhaps into town, perhaps with Yulia. And she wishes me good luck for my military service. Good luck . . . I can't see what that's got to do with anything but I thank her politely. I'm French and I've got a whole national reputation to maintain in the field of courtesy.

I'm now trying to get hold of Freddy, Rahel's boyfriend. He's tall and very broad-shouldered and he's got green eyes which always make you feel he's really listening to the person he's talking to. I adore him. Rahel tenses the minute she hears me say that, but it's true, and I can't see any harm in it. Freddy enlisted eight months ago into the Engineers. He was singled out as the most brilliant soldier in his intake. But once he'd shown his abilities and proved his excellence in six months of lessons, he couldn't tolerate continuing to take orders which he sometimes thought were stupid. So he deserted, which means he came home one Friday evening, a couple of weeks ago, and didn't set back off again on the Sunday morning. The army are not looking for him very energetically at the moment, and as for us, we're making the most of having him here, of his car, his talents in the kitchen and his lovely clear voice which sings better in Hebrew than anyone else. It's hardly surprising – he was born here, it's his own language, he instinctively puts the emphasis in the right place without worrying about the number of syllables or the structure of the word. He's the big brother I would like to have had. For years now I've felt that would have solved all my problems.

But no one's answering at Freddy's house and I hang up, disappointed. Where are they all? Why has Yulia – and, even more so, why has Rahel – chosen this particular day to disappear into thin air? This particular afternoon when I need them, it should go without saying, but no, I'd have done better to have told them, 'Right, girls, I'm heading off to the army on the 19th of September. If it's not a problem for you, I wouldn't mind if you were around on the 18th. You never know, I might want to have a bit of a chat with you. I mean, if you've got better things to do, don't even hesitate, pretend I'm not even here, I certainly wouldn't want to impinge on your freedom, I know how important it is. In less than twenty-four hours I won't have any at all . . .'

I go out for a walk round the block in case they're on the lawn, on a bench, chatting happily and not even thinking about me. Nobody. I go back up to the apartment to get my racket and balls, and I go and play against the wall at the sports club, just opposite my apartment block. After an hour of scorching direct shots, I decide I've beaten myself 6–4, 6–4, 7–5. The last shot struck me as contentious but I didn't dispute it.

Mum greets me with a wide smile.

'Where've you been? Your sister rang from her base to wish you good luck. She's really sorry, they won't let her out this evening.'

Sonia has been in the air force for a year, at a massive base seven kilometres from here. It's a five-star base, as they all are in the air force. Pilots are demi-gods. They're provided with tennis courts, swimming pools, cinemas, music rooms and a supermarket. Sonia's having a great time. She has regular leave and the rest of the time she leads a proper life in her luxury base. She also reckons that you have to hope you get lucky.

'I went to play a bit of tennis on my own. Didn't anyone else ring, apart from Sonia?'

'No.'

'Not Rahel, or Yulia or Freddy?'

'No, no one.'

Piqued, I feel seriously piqued. I know that sounds odd but it's what I feel like saying. Mum's worried.

'Is something wrong?'

'No, no, *everything's fine*.' (And I say it in English, because when I do that it makes me feel more detached, less vulnerable.)

'How was Extrapharm?'

'*Perfect, absolutely perfect*. They blew up balloons, popped balloons, stuck garlands all over the storeroom. It was great, I felt like a three-year-old.'

'You're so cynical . . .'

'No I'm not!'

'Yes, you are! When you speak in English you're being cynical. I know you inside out!'

'First of all, I've changed a bit since I was a baby. Secondly, this isn't the moment to be making jokes. Thirdly, are you cooking this evening or is Dad?'

'It'll be your father. He thought pizza, is that OK?'

'*That's perfect, abso*—'

I lunge at the telephone which has decided to ring. A happy voice on the other end says, 'Valérie? How are you, my sweet?'

What is this habit people have of not saying who they are on the phone! It really annoys me, I mean really annoys me! Do they think I've got a videophone implanted in my left hemisphere?

'I haven't got a videophone implanted in my left hemisphere,' I say. 'Who is it?'

'You're such a joker! It's Catherine (one of Mum's friends). I was just calling to wish you good luck and to comfort your mother, poor thing. She must be so sad . . . Two girls in the army . . .'

'No, she isn't sad, she couldn't be happier. I mean, tonight she can bury her life as a young mother. If you want to see her, she'll be clubbing at midnight. You see, she's getting rid of us at last. Eighteen years, that's more than enough time to get to know your children.'

I get a rather embarrassed laugh in reply. Mum throws me a black look. I hand her the phone with a shrug and shut myself in my room. I'll turn the next person who wishes me good luck into bolognaise sauce.

Shlomo Artzi is singing to me, telling me he's a soldier and that I shouldn't cry, me, the little girl. I suddenly think that in all, I mean absolutely *all* the songs about the army, it's about a boy soldier, never a girl soldier. As if I needed an extra reason to be depressed, there it is: spend two years in the army, girls, but for pity's sake be discreet! Whatever you do, don't put in an appearance in any songs!

It's 6.30.

When Jean-David left-dumped-abandoned-destroyed me I realised that you could touch rock bottom without actually dying of it. I open a book at random, to read a sentence without knowing what went before, and then to read it in context so that it feels like bumping into a old friend, a reassuring old friend. I can't believe it.

And he left, like that, with so much hidden meaning. I went home and I had the most terrible anxiety attack for no reason: those are the best. What I mean is that sort of pre-natal anxiety with no specific explanation is the most profound, the most valid, the only sort you can deem to be real. It derives from the very depths of the problem.

I'm still not sure I agree with it, but it's well said.

The phone rings, rings again, and then again. Each time I jump, Mum doesn't even bother making a move towards it. My grandmother, my aunt, my uncle, my sister, they all ring and lavish me with words of encouragement like I'm some great sportswoman before a decisive competition, like I'm a condemned man going off to serve his sentence. How kind. But I'm waiting for different phone calls. Not with much conviction now, but still hoping for them all the same.

It's at about seven o'clock that I'm getting ready to burst into tears. I've got this great lump in my throat and it's going to have to break out. The intercom buzzes. It's probably my dad who's remembered I have to go to bed early in order to be fresh, rested and serene in the morning, so he's finally coming to make his pizza which I'll eat without any appetite, all sad and knotted. I go and answer unenthusiastically.

'Yes?'

I hear some incomprehensible noises, then a chorus.

'IT'S US!'

Them? Yes, it's them! In that mixture of voices I recognised Rahel, Yulia and Freddy. They've rushed up the stairs and they're already here, with their arms full of trays and presents, and they're kissing me and hugging me.

. 'So, did you think we'd forgotten you?' Rahel asks me with a conspiratorial smile.

'No, no, not at all . . .'

'Liar!' Yulia flashes at me, tapping me gently on the nose. 'You're about as believable as Pinocchio!'

'No, really, I'd guessed you'd lay on a surprise for me! I was quietly reading my book, waiting for you to show up . . .'

I don't have time to finish my sentence before bursting into tears. It's hardly appropriate, but I can't help myself, it's happened of its own accord. They huddle round me and get me to sit down on the sofa.

'She's very emotional,' says Ilana, who's there too.

'Don't worry, I've brought just the thing,' replies Ilan, brandishing his guitar.

'Come on then, let the party begin!' Freddy cries, uncovering the trays laden with cheese pasties, pizzas and savoury pancakes.

'I've been working all day with my two assistants,' he adds, affectionately putting his arms round Rahel's and Yulia's necks.

A bright flash. It's Mum taking a picture. And she should, they look so good, the three of them, their eyes lit up by their smiles and their friendship, and by the pleasure they've taken in preparing this surprise for me. Suddenly, I'm finding breathing much more comfortable. We eat, we drink, we talk about how I'm feeling, me, the first girl in our group to go off to the army.

'I'm frightened,' I say, 'I'm scared to death. And I can't sit still for a minute. I can't wait for tomorrow, to know what they want to do with me.'

'You won't know much,' Freddy tells me. 'You'll only find out which base you'll be doing your course in, and which girls will be in the same tent as you. Courses, especially for girls, are like a precursor to the army, a preface. Loads of stuff goes on there which has nothing to do with what happens afterwards.'

'Take things as they come,' says Ilan. 'You can't make any decisions, anyway. They choose what you do and where you belong, you'll be one among others, you'll be one tiny part of Tsahal*.'

'Leave her alone,' Rahel intervenes. 'You're upsetting her with your two-bit worldly wisdom!'

'God, it seems like yesterday that you first set foot in school,' Yulia murmurs, gazing mistily. 'You didn't speak a word of Hebrew and you tried to make yourself understood in English but your French accent made everyone laugh, so no one really listened to you. You seemed so foreign, so lost . . . And now you speak as well as we do, you like the same music as us, and you're heading off for the army like us . . .'

We're all thinking about those hours of discussions when we set the world to rights, when we argued vehemently because we didn't have the same political opinions. The

* Acronym for the Israeli defence army.

rubbish parties, the brilliant parties, the schmaltzy Hollywood films and the Woody Allen films, the American series we watched without missing a single episode, the Shlomo Artzi concerts, the incredible gossip we exchanged every couple of days at school or late in the evening on the phone, under the furious glare of our parents who were seriously thinking about setting up an organisation to abolish three-hour phone calls. The pub crawls in Beersheva, Tel Aviv or Jaffa, the first tequila slammers, the first times (you know what I mean) in order: myself, then Rahel, then lastly Yulia with a Dutchman who was a volunteer on a kibbutz where she spent a couple of weeks. The sad, happy or philosophical drunken evenings, the books we started to write in the hopes of being recognised as brilliant young novelists (Yulia and myself), the books we cried over, the things that brought the boys and girls together, the things that drove them apart, is friendship possible between a girl and a boy (Freddy and myself), the *bac*, for which we still don't have our results and which we couldn't care less about this evening, the eternal loves that last just a few days, the trips to Eilat by the Red Sea, 40° in the shade, Rahel smothering herself in factor 90 sun cream, Yulia and myself scarcely skimming ourselves with factor 4 every three hours to give us delicious tans, our skin raw in the evening, painful at the least contact, Rahel's moralising glances. The little expressions in French and Russian that we've learned over the years: '*Kak dilla? Haracho. Ya hatchou damoï. Ya tibia lioublou. Spakoïne notche. Pajalousta! Shto ti hotchitch? Kto ta koya? Priviet. Comment ça va? Ça va bien. Je t'aime, mon amour. On ira où tu voudras quand tu voudras. Je vois la vie en rose'*, the questions, the answers, the doubts, the ridiculous teachers, the fascinating ones. Our lives, our teenage years unfurl before our eyes and we experience an unfamiliar feeling, something sweet but sad which weighs on our hearts: for the first time we have a tremendous feeling of nostalgia.

'How about opening your presents?' Rahel suggests, and she, like the rest of us, has slightly moist eyes, but she's not that keen to give in to all this sentimentality.

They form a circle around me, watching my reactions which I'm sure they've predicted.

My more distant friends, like Ilan and Ilana, have gone for the classics: raspberry-scented shower gel, earrings, a make-up set. Rahel, Yulia and Freddy have grouped together to give me something really special or a real surprise. A Danny Robas album (he's posing a serious threat to Shlomo Artzi in the top ten at the moment), some poems by Yonatan Geffen, the most sensitive and ironic of our poet-journalist-writers, and a sort of joke survival kit with loads of little packets which I have to open in a particular order. In each of them there's an explanatory note:

A packet of condoms for emergency situations of affection

Two packets of tissues for evenings of serious depression

Leg-waxing kit which must be used before the emergency affection

Aspirins to soothe my pig-headed head

A torch to see the light at the end of the tunnel

A big T-shirt with the words 'two-year holiday' printed on it to give me sweet dreams

A clown nose so that I can laugh at least once a day when I look at myself in the mirror

25 phone tokens to ring them at midnight to say, 'I just have to tell you this . . .'

A little photo album with the 'best of' our photos so that I never forget I've got friends who are always there.

I say thank you, I kiss them, I solemnly decorate them with medals for being the best friends in the world. Ilan starts strumming on his guitar and sings a song by the Russian Vladimir Vissotski. Then we sing in Hebrew while Mum takes pictures of us from every angle. I feel good. Tomorrow's no longer palpable.

TO ARMS, ETC.

Mum wakes me more gently than usual. It's half past six, I have to be at the recruitment office in two hours.

'Mmm . . . it's early,' I mumble. 'Let me sleep a bit longer.'

'No,' she retorts firmly. 'You shouldn't set off for the army in a hurry.'

I extricate myself from the sheets, my head a little heavy. I know I dreamt about Jean-David: he was in a whirlwind and I couldn't get close to it. He had that permanent ironic smile on his lips and he didn't notice my initial efforts or my eventual distress. Then there was a gunshot, but it may only have been the sound of the door as Mum came into my room.

I slip to the bathroom and it feels as if I'm an automaton. How can a body make all sorts of manoeuvres when the brain isn't engaged, when it's inert? I promise myself I'll try and find a book on the subject. I work on the reassuring principle that all the answers can be found in books.

Mum has concocted a five-star breakfast. Pancakes, yoghurt with maple syrup, real hot chocolate, freshly squeezed orange juice: she must have got up at five o'clock to get it all ready, wanting to make me happy but not realising that it would look to me like a condemned man's last meal – condemned woman in this instance. I'm being given the best before being sent to confront the worst. I'm exaggerating. Let's say that right now I'm about to confront the unknown, which is definitely frightening enough for a start.

Having finished my feast, I go down for a short walk round the block. I walk slowly past the benches, the swings, the little areas of lawn. Then I go round the corner of our building and gaze for a long time at our school standing out against the desert; next I look at Yulia's window, then Rahel's. I imprint each detail on myself, taking a snapshot of the setting for my adolescence, just as I took in the countryside of my childhood before leaving France five years ago.

Freddy offered to drive me to the recruitment office. I reminded him that he was considered a deserter and that it might not be the most welcoming of places towards him. He laughed as he replied that his picture wasn't hanging in every military base on 'Wanted' posters. He added that throwing yourself into the wolf's jaws was the best way of avoiding its gaze. I could tell that Rahel was worried, but she didn't say anything.

At eight o'clock they're all there.

Ilan, who's just passed his driving test, has come in his mother's car. Two cars isn't overdoing it: there are ten friends

accompanying me. It's a presidential escort, an unprece-
dented homage, anointed by the people! They form a guard of
honour and give me a military salute. I feel more and more
like I'm going to cry, like yesterday. My tear ducts are on full
output, they're even doing unpaid overtime. I'm the *Grande
Dame* of tear duct operations.

Freddy puts Shlomo Artzi on full volume. *But I'm a
soldier, don't cry little girl*, and we drown his voice out,
bellowing, *But I'm a soldier girl, don't cry little boy*. Behind
us, Ilan hoots his horn in time to whatever they're listening
to. It's no longer a fanfare, it's an experiment to test the
locals' tolerance to sound levels. But no one reacts. They
know the autumn's the peak season for harvesting, and that
the crop is eighteen-year-olds.

Outside the recruitment office it's like a cattle market of
soldiers. People are shouting, hugging, laughing, crying. The
girls who are leaving, like me, are easy to spot: they're
surrounded by circles of friends and relations, hanging round
their boyfriends' necks. The warmth surrounding them is
palpable. A dose of friendship, one last ration of love, a kiss
for Daddy, a kiss for Mummy, a kiss for the little brother
standing in mute admiration (there's one of six or seven
dressed up as a soldier: everyone's looking at him adoringly;
I look away, embarrassed).

The parents are recognisable too: they're forty-five years
old rather than twenty, of course, but most noticeably they're
the ones with tears in their eyes, looking both proud and
anxious. They slip each other conspiratorial looks. They

seem to understand each other without speaking.

The press are there. When they're approached by photographers, most of the girls adopt poses which are meant to be natural, hoping to be in the paper the next day with the caption: 'Countdown to the Army' or 'A Kiss Before Khaki'.

I automatically take my glasses off. Yulia is fluttering her eyelashes *prestissimo*.

'Friends and rivals for ever,' I mutter to myself.

Suddenly a ripple runs through the crowd. A soldier who thinks he's the Chief of Staff, or at least a replica of Rambo, has just stepped up on to the running board of one of the line of buses purring, ready to go. He eyes the crowd for a few seconds, a triumphant sadistic smile on his lips. He's brimming with happiness, a happiness conferred on him by these few moments of power over all these girls devouring him with their eyes, as if he held their lives in his hands, when he's actually only got a wodge of paper which he's leafing through with affected nonchalance. Silence descends. He scratches his throat and starts his little performance.

I feel as if it's 1914 and I'm part of the general mobilisation.

'Ladies, gentlemen and soldiers! We shall now proceed with drawing lots . . . No, I'm joking. When I call out your name, please get on to the bus and give me your call-up number. Could I ask you not to draw out your goodbyes, it's a health hazard . . . and it won't help you lose weight.'

Yulia sniggers contemptuously.

I wish I could react like her and to say out loud that he's a stupid prick. But I'm terrified at the thought that this is the first idiot in uniform I've come across on this long journey, and he certainly won't be the last.

'And he's ugly, too,' says Rahel, to comfort me.

'You see, he's a *jobnik**,' Freddy whispers. 'Have a good look at him and you'll be able to recognise them all. I don't know why, they have a family resemblance.'

'Stupidity *is* a family resemblance,' Ilan flashes sententiously.

The jobnik glowers at us. Given the distance between us, he can't have heard anything, but the simple fact that we're talking is an assault on the mute respect he expects from us. He starts his litany.

'Avneri, Tali . . .'

A chubby little thing with frizzy hair bursts into tears and hugs her mother compulsively. The crowd parts to let them pass, and it's as if a signal has been given: the effusive good-byes start up again all the louder, making such a din that the jobnik's nasal voice has a job making itself heard.

'Berrebi, Ronit . . .'

I kiss everyone ten times with a feeling of hopeless urgency. They say all sorts of kind things which jumble together so that I don't really hear them.

My parents are at the height of their emotion, their tears are flowing.

'I promised myself I wouldn't cry,' Mum apologises, 'I didn't want to . . .'

'It doesn't matter,' I whisper in her ear, 'you can't be different from the others. And anyway, at the end of the day, it

---

* A term used to describe useless people who are stuck in safe, boring jobs.

60

doesn't matter how early you get up, you always set off for the army in a hurry.'

She smiles through her tears. Dad hugs me very tight and whispers something which sounds like 'look after yourself'. My friends keep saying things which are intended to make me laugh.

In Hebrew, the letter Z is the seventh in the alphabet. It won't be long before I hear my name.

'Varchavski, Tami . . . Zenatti, Valérie . . .'

I bite my lip, try to keep my balance with my three-ton bag, and I hand my call-up papers to the mega-twat, who's already calling out the next name as he takes them.

I choose the last free window seat. The crowd has huddled round the bus, there are people gesticulating their love, their goodbyes and their encouragement. Our bus fills up very quickly, the door slides shut, it sets off, and the faces disappear too soon.

I settle into my seat and close my eyes.

It's over. And it's just beginning.

The bus is already out of town, rumbling across the desert towards Tel Aviv. It's a road I've taken dozens of times but today I feel as if I don't know where it goes. I've taken my personal stereo out. I want to listen to the Danny Robas album my friends have given me.

An elbow digs me in the ribs and tears me away from the music, which already feels like my own personal hymn. I take my earphones off. The girl next to me gives me a reproachful look.

'Do you think you're on a trip to Eilat, sweetheart? Don't you know you're a soldier now?'

'So what's the problem?'

'The problem? It's about two rows of seats away from us, is about 1m70 and looks a bit like a bullock, but not so bright. He's in charge of us until we get to the reception base.'

'OK! So what?'

'He's just said we're not allowed personal stereos.'

'But it's not as if we're in a plane that's taking off!' I retort, furious.

'I dunno, I've never been on a plane. But what I do know is that you'd better come down to land otherwise you're not going to get very far like that. You're going to walk straight into deep trouble.'

'You fill me with optimism. You're the angel of good tidings.'

'And I can already tell you're going to be fun. You're not like the others. It's like you landed up here by chance. A bit like, like . . .' She's trying to find a simile, and I generously decide to help.

'Like bird shit?'

Her eyes widen with surprise.

'You must be from the planet Doolally,' she protests. 'It's just been identified as part of our solar system.'

'Yes, that's right. You're very sharp, angel of good tidings. And to be absolutely straight with you, I've come to spy on the second most powerful army in the world, or is it the fourth, I don't remember . . .'

'You'll get what you came for. If they're all like this bullock that you and your friends were taking the mickey out of so viciously earlier, you're going to have trouble understanding how powerful Tsahal is.'

'You're wrong there, you poor human with so little imagination. It's not the bullocks or even the boys that I'm studying. It's the army in its entirety. Full stop, new paragraph.'

'Hey, you've got a mega-sophisticated computer in your brain!' she hisses, full of admiration. 'I hope we won't be separated straightaway when we get to the reception base. Do you have any idea yet what they're going to be doing with you?'

'Mmmm . . . yes . . . maybe. In the last year I've been called up four times for psycho-thingummy tests. For the intelligence service, apparently. But there's nothing definite . . .'

'Wow! I've stumbled across a serious IQ!'

I nod my head, completely in agreement with her. It's time I showed some interest in her.

'And do you know where you're going? Do you know what you'd like to do?'

'Yup. It's mapped out already. I'm going to be a sports instructor.'

I'm bowled over by so much conviction. I look at her more closely. We're both sitting down but I get the feeling we're the same height, round about 1m64. She is quite muscular, from what I can see of her arms and legs. Her chestnut hair is very short, a spiky cut that's been really fashionable for about a year. I don't know why but I've always thought that girls with that sort of haircut are very sure of themselves, sporty and sociable. Comfortable with themselves, in other words. She has square features, clear skin and green eyes, all screwed up as if she's been making fun of the world all her life, and always will. She inspires confidence in me. I also hope we won't be separated at the reception base.

'I should inform you, to expand your general knowledge, that my name's Valérie Zenatti.'

'Delighted, *enchantée*, my respects . . . And you have the enormous privilege of addressing Eynat Haymovitch.'

'I don't know what to say . . . hey, do you think we're also not allowed to sleep?'

'The little bullock didn't say anything about that.'

'Well, if you'll excuse me, I'm going to have to close my eyes. I get this feeling it's not going to be possible very often over the next few days.'

'You speak words of great truth, Valérie Zenatti. Allow me to follow suit.'

I agree and close my eyes. In my half-sleep, I feel our heads resting against each other. I find it reassuring.

The nasal voice, amplified by a microphone, wakes us sharply.

'Soldiers! We're about to go through the gates to the reception base. You'll spend the day here. You'll be given your belongings and you'll carry out all the formalities for enrolling. Then you'll be sent to a training base where you'll have all your classes.'

A girl at the back of the bus puts up her hand and asks shakily, 'Are we really going to be given vaccinations?'

A peal of laughter runs through the rows of seats. With

tears in her eyes, the girl apologises and mutters that she's terrified of needles.

The bullock confirms the sorry news and adds, 'I hope you'll give the best of yourselves over these two years.'

Eynat leans over and whispers, 'He forgot to say goodbye and good riddance.'

I smile at her. I look out of the window. We're at the barrier by the entrance to the base. There are white boards attached to the barbed wire fencing. 'Secure army ground. No photography. All offenders will be punished by law.'

I've already seen dozens of boards like this: Israel's a very small country, and you can hardly step outside your back door without stumbling across army ground. But, like all the girls in the bus, I've never known what was lurking behind the barbed wire. My heart beats a little faster, with impatience and fear. This is one of the biggest bases in Israel, right next to Tel Aviv. Every soldier, boy or girl, who has done military service has spent at least two days of their life in this place. The first day of their service and the day of their release.

There's a soldier on duty at the entrance. He looks monumentally bored. He vaguely inspects our bus, says a few words to our chaperone and waves us past. The bus rolls on for several more minutes, then stops in front of a row of prefabricated buildings. There's a young woman waiting for us. She's an officer, judging by the two metal stripes on her epaulettes. Our guide gets off the bus and gives her a regulation salute. I get the feeling that this little performance is meant to impress us. The officer returns the salute.

We get off.

'Good morning, girls! I'm Major Sarit Nigun, I'm in charge of reception and training. Call me "Major" and nothing else. This is definitely the last time you will be thought of as "girls": today you will become soldiers, and when you take off your uniform in two years' time, if everything goes as it should, you will be young women.'

'This isn't a welcome speech, it's a funeral oration,' I whisper to Eynat.

'She didn't make it clear if deflowering was included in the price,' she whispers back.

'You will have to get used to some rules straightaway,' Major Sarit continues. 'Rule number one: you don't ask any questions, except in emergencies. Everything you are asked or told to do has been thought out at great length by competent, responsible people. Any order from someone of higher rank than yourselves must be carried out, except, of course, for those that involve murder, betrayal or sexual abuse.'

Sniggering pretty much all round.

'Rule number two: you do not laugh, you do not talk – in fact you don't move a muscle when you're being spoken to. No one is here for their own entertainment. A more complete set of general rules will be given to each of you in your training bases. You will now be given your regimental numbers and your military papers. Then, you will be vaccinated.'

My companions clamp their mouths shut. I wonder whether they're afraid of the injections or if they're shuddering at the thought of showing their bums off to everyone.

Personally, I'm not really taken with either of them.

'You will have lunch here, then your uniforms will be handed out. I'll take this opportunity to tell you about rule number three: the loss or theft of any item of clothing, piece of equipment, weapon or other object belonging to the army is punished with imprisonment ranging from one week to several years. Right, back to today. When you've changed into your uniforms, you will be given a posting to a training base. You will be taken there by bus, and it is there that you will officially begin your military service. For now, follow me.'

We meekly form a single file. Not one of us can have been as cooperative since the first year at primary school. Eynat puts herself right behind me.

We go into one of the sheds where a succession of jobniks glance at us and sneer. I know this won't be the last time we're subjected to this sort of stupid minor humiliation. We're the new girls, the 'rookies', and that's what we'll be for some time yet.

We have our photos taken for our identity papers. No time to choose a pose, straighten our hair or attempt a smile: ten seconds maximum per person.

We're each given a flat oblong tag with a line of pinpricks down the centre, hanging on an unbreakable chain, and we're told that it must **never*** be taken off. Our surnames, first names and regimental numbers are imprinted on it twice. We're told that in the event of accidental death or death in

---

* The bold was in the Sergeant's voice as he gave us the information.

combat, the tag makes it possible to identify the victim. If bodies cannot be removed from a battlefield, any uninjured soldiers should break the metal in two (hence the pinpricks), leave the half attached to the chain on the injured or dead soldier's body, and take the other half to the authorities who then send it on to the parents. When soldiers are taken as prisoners of war, the tag means the Red Cross can be informed of their identity.

Referring to our possible deaths casts a serious shadow over every face. I put the chain round my neck and warm the tag with my hands, horrified by this mechanical voice telling us about bodies, victims, battlefields, deaths and families being given appallingly definitive news.

I turn to Eynat.

'He could have said it in a more gentle voice, sadder, more apologetic. He spieled out all those horrors like he was talking about special promotions in a shopping centre!'

'The army isn't for poets, dear girl.'

The major starts talking again.

'Learn your regimental number by heart here this evening. It's your new i-den-ti-ty. You should be able to say it very quickly, even if you're woken in the middle of the night.'

I look at my tag: 3810159. Eynat's number is (I should say Eynat is) 3810168.

We're handed prisoner of war cards. Mine brings me up short: it's written in Hebrew and in French which, it transpires, is the international military language. This fills me with a huge feeling of joy which is a bit of surprise: it feels as if France, even though it's so far away, is giving me a friendly sign, a sign that I alone understand, and – to the amazement of the girls around me – I immerse myself with genuine interest in the summary of the principal articles from the Geneva Convention which is printed on the back of the card.

Then the vaccinations, the pain, because we're so tense we could almost die, twenty of us together in the room with our bums in the air.

Then the meal, in a huge refectory. Holding our trays we file past soldiers on fatigue duty who nudge each other, exchange knowing glances and double up laughing. There's something I don't understand: if we'd met these boys or girls somewhere else, we'd have chatted quite normally, as equals. But in this base we have roles to play, we represent one group (the new intake) confronted with another (the old hands), and it doesn't really matter who we actually are, every element of the one has to take the mickey out of the other. I confess to Eynat what I'm thinking, expecting some sarcastic remark. But that's not what happens: she actually nods seriously. But we're already being taken off to do something else, to get the thing we've all been waiting for impatiently, the thing which has been fuelling our conversations with our girlfriends for the last few months: the uniform.

I think we're all secretly hoping for it to bring about a metamorphosis, give us a little extra seductiveness, confidence, sense of identity. Our hands scrabble impatiently with the packaging. Inside: a huge jute bag (the soldier's kitbag), two long-sleeved shirts, one short-sleeved shirt in stiff cotton, a big itchy sweater, two pairs of trousers, a skirt cut like a sack of potatoes, a Michelin man anorak, a black forage cap with the Tsahal insignia, a shoulder bag (also black with two phosphorescent strips so that you can be seen at night), and some incredibly 1950s shoes, which are generally known as 'Golda' shoes after Golda Meir* who used at least eighty-two pairs of them in her life, and who was about as interested in fashion as a nineteenth-century Ukrainian peasant woman.

We're warned that we must make absolutely no alterations to the clothing, because we might be posted to the marines or the air force which have grey uniforms. As for our weapons, equipment and battledress, we'll be given those in our training bases.

We get dressed in record time and the excitement reaches a peak in front of the only mirror in the room. Astonishment, shudders of emotion, pleasure in dressing up, like when you put Mummy's shoes on when you're little.

Time is speeding by faster and faster.

We're told to hurry up, get out and line up in squares of five by five, to be given our identity papers and then, finally, to get into the bus. The girls who know each other keep catching each other's eyes hopefully. I clench my fists tightly, stupidly hoping that this demonstration of strength will mean Eynat will be posted to the same base as me.

So, it's the roll call once again. I wait for my military number, I give my new friend a little wave and make my way slowly over to the bus with a lump in my throat. Then I

* Israeli Prime Minister from 1969 to 1974.

nearly fall flat in the dust as 65kg comes crashing into me. 65kg which, at a rough guess, represents the combination of Eynat's 55kg and the 10kg of her kitbag.

We're on the road. I'm in uniform, sitting next to a girl I already feel really close to, and she's in uniform too. I look at my watch.

Scarcely ten hours have passed since this morning.

NUMBER 3810159
REGIMENT 3, COMPANY D

I take a notebook from my bag. On the cover I've written simply: *Girl soldier: 19th September – ?* The question mark is either there to reassure me or to frighten me, I don't really know. Either way, it's not sure of the future.

I want to make scrupulous notes on the events of the day, and particularly what I've been feeling. I feel that if I don't write down what I'm doing on a daily basis it's as if nothing's happening. I've felt like that since I was twelve. The only year I wrote nothing was when I came to Israel: too many discoveries and emotions and new people – every minute was intense. And this language, Hebrew, which made the whole outside world incomprehensible, obscure. I don't remember anything from that year, it's like a big gap in my memory. Even if I try, nothing comes, it's total black-out.

Today's a bit like that, it's taken just a few hours to

catapult me into an alien world. So, in spite of or because of the ruts in the road, here I am writing sentences without subjects, without verbs, just isolated adjectives.

The jobniks, depressing. The grub, hardly appetising. The world's turned all grey and khaki. Even the eucalyptus trees look as if they've been planted to complement the grey-green colour scheme. A bit earlier, the uniform. Excitement. It's stupid, but I feel different, and I'm not the only one. We're all talking differently since we put it on. Can't wait to see myself in a full-length mirror, head to foot.

Eynat. A friend? A nice girl, anyway.

Everything's going too quickly, much too quickly.

It's dark and Eynat's gone to sleep. We're travelling towards Hadera, to the north of Tel Aviv. A quick glance at the moon, round and bright, and I too fall asleep.

The bus jolts, bounces, splutters. We've left the motorway and we're on a badly kept little road. A succession of bumps and ruts. Clearly, we're being shown that we're not here to be cosseted. In the half-light I can make out the barbed wire fences round the base, the checkpoint guarded by two soldiers, and the huge silhouettes of the eucalyptus trees with shadows blacker than the night. A remake of this morning, the unlit night-time version.

We're asked to get off the bus with our belongings, including our huge kitbags which are at least 1m20 high. The little brunette who's terrified of vaccinations can't be much taller than 1m50, and you can hardly see her above her load. I smile.

'Why are you smiling at the bus?' Eynat asks, surprised.

I tilt my chin towards Tali (if I've remembered her name right).

'Look. I feel sorry for her. She looks like a kitbag on feet with a few frizzy bits of hair on top. She reminds me of Laurel and Hardy films, or Charlie Chaplin. D'you see what I mean?'

'Not really. I must have watched a few when I was little, but everyone thought they were old hat, pre-war . . .'

'They're not "old hat",' I protest, 'they're all about little guys, fat guys, the naive, the clumsy, losers, people who disappear behind big kitbags.'

'Do you like losers, then, is that it?'

I'm struck dumb by the question. I've always been THE first at everything, right through school, in music, in tennis*. So I'm obviously not a loser. But I do find people who lose moving.

I don't have time to explain all this to Eynat, or to myself. An incredibly beautiful girl has just appeared before us. Short brown hair, very olive complexion, a perfectly sculpted face, wearing battledress which looks as if it were tailored by Yves Saint Laurent and a wide-brimmed cap clamped on her head. She has a short M16 slung across her; it's the most chic weapon in the army, reserved for officers. The two stripes on her epaulettes indicate that she's a lieutenant.

'Lieutenant Inbar Katz,' she introduces herself. 'I'm your regimental commander. Put your bags against the wall and line up in columns of five, please.'

---

* But, to be honest, never in athletics or swimming.

She doesn't raise her voice, there's nothing unpleasant or even cold about her tone. It's neutral, with a hint of sympathy. She clearly knows that she only has to be there and to open her mouth in order to be obeyed by a hundred or so girls. I suddenly feel very, very ugly, with an IQ of –10. I lean towards Eynat.

'Do you think she's an agent paid by the Syrians to demoralise Israeli soldiers?'

'Maybe . . . it's incredible, everyone obeys her instantly. She's got a hell of a lot of charisma . . .'

' . . . And we look so bloody stupid with our stiff, spanking new uniforms which stink of starch from 200 paces.'

Inbar Katz is standing bolt upright in front of us, between four girls a little younger than herself, in other words not much older than us, and they too are wearing wide-brimmed caps.

'Welcome to Base 80. For the next four weeks you will have your classes here in Regiment 3. This regiment is made up of four companies, each under the authority of one of the four corporals here. They will proceed with the roll call, and take you to your tents.'

She suddenly changes the tone of her voice to call, 'Corporal Tamar!'

The tallest of the girls takes three steps forward, makes a quarter-turn, three steps to the left, another quarter-turn, one step forward, and brings her hand briskly up to her forehead. It's the first real military salute I've seen, and I'm impressed.

'Call the soldiers for A Company!'

'Yes, ma'am.'

Military salute again. The corporal turns towards us and reads out her list, and I'm beginning to get to know the numbers. I jump slightly when I hear Eynat's, and she winks at me as she goes to pick up her things. Corporal Tamar puts the list back into her pocket, turns to the officer, salutes again and says, 'There are twenty soldiers in the company, ma'am.'

'Good. Dismissed.'

The group moves away. I've been separated from Eynat but I don't feel upset. There's too much excitement. In a few minutes I too will be integrated into this world which is so serious, coded and organised. I've forgotten all my fears, my heart's pumping away, I'm thrilled, as if I've just been told I've got the lead role in a mega-production called something like *Soldier Girl* or *Gun in Hand*. I can already hear the title music.

Another corporal has started the same procedure as the first, but she doesn't call out my number either. Then it's the third one's turn, and finally the last, Corporal Kineret with curly blonde hair and calm blue eyes. There are only twenty of us left, but she still reads out all the numbers, and gives her report like the others. We follow her into the darkness.

She takes us to the tents, points to the two which have been allocated to us and takes charge of dividing us up.

Inside the tent there are ten camp beds with mattresses two centimetres thick – and I'm being generous with my guesswork.

'Put your things down by the beds, you've got two minutes

to get yourselves organised. Then line up outside in rows of five along with the other soldiers in the company.'

She goes out.

Bubbling excitement in the tent. Some girls who already know each other launch into a debate about the choice of beds.

I ask calmly, 'Has anyone got a watch with a second hand on it?'

They look at me, question marks flashing in their eyes.

'She said two minutes. In the army that means 120 seconds and not one more, get it? Give me a watch, and make your minds up. I'll take whichever bed's left.'

We're outside on the 118th second. The corporal is, indeed, keeping an eye on a big sports watch. She comes to stand in front of us.

'Soldiers! From now on, you will march everywhere on the base when you're under my command. Marching always starts with the left foot. You must be perfectly lined up and in step, and you must be attentive and follow the instructions "half-turn, right" and "half-turn, left". When you're in square formation, as you are now, you should be standing to attention until you hear the order "At ease". Keep your heels together and stand absolutely upright however long the formation is maintained. Every day I will name one of you head of company. She will have to give a report on numbers at every roll call, I will give her the list of tasks for the company, and she will be responsible for reveille and for respecting the timetable. *She* will suffer the consequences if you're late. On to other things: when you're on the base if you come across someone of a higher rank than yourselves you must salute them, like this.' Her right hand, tilted at 45°, comes up to just above her right eyebrow. 'We're going to get your sheets, blankets and fatigues. D Company, attention!'

We stand to attention.

'Half-turn, left!'

We pivot round as one woman.

'Left, right, left, right, left, right . . .'

The little group sets off. Some have trouble keeping in step, and skip to keep in line with the others.

'D Company, halt!'

Everyone stops dead. Some girls even have one leg still in the air. It's like a children's game, but there's no enchanted forest or fluffy squirrels. We're in front of a prefabricated building. Like in the reception base – and like everywhere else, if you ask me – no one's agonised over the architecture.

'D Company, go into the block in single file.'

We take two blankets in an indefinable colour and as scratchy as the sweaters. Then we give our clothes and shoe size. We're handed two sets of rather crumpled fatigues, ridiculous little hats with the word Tsahal on them in yellow, and a pair of lace-up ankle boots, which are way more flattering than the Golda shoes.

'D Company, attention! Left, right, left, right, left, right . . .'

Back to the tents where we have all of five minutes to change and put our things away.

In square formation again, in front of the tents. Attention. At ease. Left, right, left, right, left, right. Destination: the centre of the base. We come across other companies, marching like us. We glance at each other, trying to recognise faces, but it's difficult, everyone's wearing a hat.

'D Company, halt!'

We come to a halt in front of what must be the canteen, judging by the smells. There are at least five companies waiting their turn. My boots are rubbing my feet. The hat, which is too tight, is already giving me a migraine. And I'm hungry.

After a quarter of an hour standing still, without breathing a word, of course, D Company is invited to go into the canteen. From that moment we have twenty minutes. That's a directive from headquarters, and everyone is subject to it. Twenty minutes to eat and six hours' sleep a day, those are a soldier's fundamental rights, and their only rights, as far as I can see.

On the menu: tomato salad, grilled corned beef, boiled carrots. The whole lot is served on one plate, which gets little gasps of disgust from us. Then we're shown to a long table which is already partly occupied (a soldier on duty has told us that we have to fill up the empty places systematically).

Most of the girls hardly touch what's on their plates and launch straight into the yoghurt on the table. I lay into mine with some enthusiasm, under their reproachful glances. I ask them whether they're hoping to hold out for three weeks on hunger strike, but they don't answer. They watch me with friendly expressions.

'By the way, are you French?'

'Yes.'

'Wow! You're so lucky!'

'Tell us about Paris!'

'Say something in French!'

'Sing *Au clair de la lune*!'

Here we go again. But they seem so happy that I do as I'm asked willingly. And I say something like 'We're all gorgeous in our uniforms and we're going to have a great time here' in French, and then start on the first verse of *Au clair de la lune* as they watch contentedly. It's surreal: here I am, a soldier in fatigues, about to spend the night in a tent, tomorrow I'll probably be carrying a weapon . . . and I'm singing a French lullaby!

It's already time to clear our trays, which we put down on to a conveyor belt.

No surprises: square formation, attention, left, right, left, right, left, right, half-turn left, left, right, left, right. D Company: halt.

'You now have half an hour until lights out. The showers and toilets are in a shed three tents down from here. Tonight, as an exception, you won't be doing any guard duties. Reveille tomorrow morning will be at half past four. At five o'clock your tent should be immaculate and you should be in square formation. Who's number 3810254?'

A girl smothered in freckles puts her hand up.

'Right. You're in charge of the group as from now and for the next twenty-four hours. You will count your fellow soldiers tomorrow and give me a report, do you understand?'

Number 3810254 brings her hand up to her temple.

'Yes.'

'You must say "Yes, ma'am".'

'Yes, ma'am.'

'Good. Do you have any questions for the group as a whole?'

The newly appointed group leader ventures, 'Can we make phone calls?'

'There are two phone booths for you over by the refectory. They take phone tokens. But remember! Your phone calls mustn't dig into your sleep time. Any more questions?'

Our silence is her answer.

'OK! D Company, dismissed! Goodnight.'

Given how short the night's going to be, I take it that's sarcasm.

The company is a hive of activity again. A dozen or so girls bound into the tents and look frantically for their stocks of telephone tokens. Others, because they're more hygienic or more independent, head towards the shower block, toothbrush and soap in hand.

I stay by myself. Hesitating. There are some choices I've never been able to make.

Like the others, I feel like telling someone about my day. I know that, back home, they're waiting impatiently for me to call. But if I go over to the phones I'll be desperate to speak to Rahel. And, while I'm at it, to Yulia. The other girls (I'm not yet resigned to calling them 'the other soldiers') would lynch me before I could dial a second number. Two phone booths! And there were 200 of us, I think, who arrived today! Quick calculation: if everyone makes a call, that would be about ten seconds per person, including dialling, connecting and ringing.

Bugger.

For years Mum went on at me, saying you had to brush your teeth for three minutes, thoroughly, top to bottom. Morning, noon and night.

Maybe, even though I've come of age and I'm in uniform, today's the day to prove once and for all that I haven't forgotten anything from my upbringing.

The climate is positively tropical in the sanitation block (sanitation – what a word!). There are about twenty girls having showers. Others are waiting their turn. There are no curtains: too expensive or unhygienic. I imagine that's the excuse that was given at some time. Unless modesty is considered a foible restricted to adolescence which has no place here.

I take my new toothbrush from its case, and stand in front of one of the fifteen taps which hang over a single long, narrow metal basin. There's a little stream – the sort you'd find in a gutter, mind you – of water whitened by a mixture of toothpaste and saliva. None of this seems to bother the girls. Several of them are singing the choruses of songs learned with Tsofim, the non-religious patriotic movement. They seem to be at ease, in their element. That must be why they've chosen the showers instead of the phone.

I'm looking for Eynat and I can't find her. I don't know which tent she's in, and I've only got twenty minutes until lights out. I'd like to read a bit and to write some more before going to sleep.

Destination D Company tent.

Three of my room-mates have collapsed on to their beds. They're nibbling biscuits and noisily discussing their fruitless trip to the phone booths. They glance over at me a few times but not enough to interrupt their conversation. I open my book.

'Hey, French girl, are you reading a tour guide on Tsahal bases?'

'Are you hoping to wrap up a doctorate in military strategy in two years?'

'Do you need to read *Little Red Riding Hood* before you go to sleep?'

The mocking comments continue to fly. I don't let it bother me. In this country, sarcastic humour and contempt are a means of communication that everyone understands. A language within the language. A way of confirming that you don't think the person you're talking to is fragile (which is the equivalent of depressive here), that you don't have to tiptoe round them. I'm having a go at you, so you must be one of us.

So I close my book, which is in French, and settle for thinking about France, about how we used to go to Paris in the holidays. My sister and I used to dream about it all year long. Perhaps this isn't the time to think back over the happiest moments of my childhood.

Feeling slightly guilty towards the book for having abandoned it like that, I feel I should defend reading in front of my room-mates.

'Just because we're in uniform, we don't have to be uneducated. And just because I'm French, I don't live in a fairy tale! I need to read, to remember that the outside world is there.'

I realise that this is going over the top a bit.

Pretentious, sententious (a liar, a thief, nasty, vicious, always wittering on – I automatically make out a list in my head . . . and there's little doubt it applies to me).

To compensate for my intellectual snobbery, I add, 'Or we could just pack in all this jibing? We're stuck with each other for a month. We should get to know each other . . .'

My suggestion couldn't have come at a better time. The other girls have come back from the showers and the phone booths. Smelling of lovely vanilla soap, or with their eyes reddened by a heartbreaking conversation with their mothers, I imagine. Introductions:

'Keren from Haïfa.'

'Tamar from Ashkelon.'

'Shlomit – call me Shula – from Petah Tikva.'

'Sivan – your group leader, may I remind you – from Jerusalem.'

'Riki from Kfar Saba.'

'Yaël from Revivim.'

'Dorit from Tiberiade.'

'Galit from Tel Aviv.'

'Vered from Bat Yam.'

And me.

A strange first name. From a town where I wasn't born. Their names all have an immediate, specific meaning: ray of sun, date, gazelle, little wave, rose. Or they refer to biblical characters like Rebecca (Rivka, which is shortened to Riki) or

Shlomit. They're used to names 'meaning' something, and they ask me what Valérie means in French.

'I don't know, I think it comes from Latin. But if you chop the word up you get "va et ri", and that means "go and laugh".'

This leaves them a bit perplexed. Outside someone shouts, 'Lights out! Lights out!'

Ten hands reach up to switch off the light. Voices say 'goodnight' in every direction.

It's only half past ten. It's at least five years since I've been to bed so early. I'm going to do some thinking, toss in my narrow little bed, try to find a comfortable position, run through the events of the day, I'm going to . . .

None of the above. I'm already asleep.

KEEP IN STEP!

There's something disturbing about being woken by some-one you hardly know in the dead of night (even if, as far as I can make out, morning begins at four o'clock in the army). Once out of bed, it's cold. And yet it's September. I've never been cold at this time of year in Israel. I picture some monstrous ventilating system responsible for refrigerating Tsahal bases, to teach us how tough life is.

Distinctly less talkative than last night, we put on our fatigues. If I look anything like the others, I'd better steer clear of mirrors: puffy face, yellow complexion, piggy eyes.

Sivan, who already feels accountable and responsible for our every action, is worried that some girls are putting on their sweaters and buttoning up their anoraks.

'Do you think we're *allowed* to?' she whispers.

The poor frozen things shrug their shoulders.

'We have to get up at 4.30 but no one said that on top of that we have to freeze to death. If she says anything, we'll take them off, that's all.'

So, on with the scratchy sweater and Michelin man anorak. Even a supermodel would look like an elephant in that lot. But she's not doing military service, and she'll never know how depressing it feels being a frozen, badly dressed, private soldier girl.

A khaki cohort mills round the wash basins. I see a spiky little hedgehog head, and I put my hands over her eyes. Eynat spits out her toothpaste.

'Did you sleep well?' she asks me.

'Don't ask questions that are going to upset people in the middle of the night.'

'Which tent are you in?'

'Number 13, and you?'

'Number 27. Try and come over this evening before lights out. I've got to go, I haven't made my bed.'

Neither have I. I join the girls back in the tent where they're caught up in a major debate: how should we make our beds? Some claim they know from reliable sources (brothers, fathers, boyfriends) that the sheets and blankets have to be folded; others suggest we tuck the whole thing in neatly; one girl romantically suggests we should turn the sheets down across the bed like they do in hotels. Our group leader's getting impatient, it's 4.50.

'Whatever we do, it won't be right. Kineret didn't say anything specific. Let's just make sure it's tidy. And quickly.'

At 4.58 we're in square formation. Sivan's in the first row, very nervous. Corporal Kineret turns up nonchalantly at bang on five o'clock and gives the order:

'D Company, attention!'

We bring our right hands sharply up to our foreheads. The girl on my left gives a little cry and rubs her eye: clearly, her aim went a bit wrong. I bite my lip to stop myself laughing.

'Private Sivan, your report.'

Sivan takes three steps forward, salutes again, and says (in what's meant to be a firm voice), 'There are twenty soldiers in the company, ma'am!'

'Which company?'

'D Company, ma'am.'

'You should make that clear. Stay to attention, I'm going to inspect your tents.'

Two minutes go by. She comes back without making any comment.

'D Company, half-turn left! Left, right, left, right, left, right.'

We arrive on the square where we were all gathered last night. The whole regiment is gathered, but Lieutenant Inbar Katz isn't there.

One of the corporals starts to speak.

'We'll begin our day with some warm-up exercises. Break-fast is at six o'clock. Please take off your anoraks and line up in single file.'

We pull faces . . . and shiver.

Then, under the corporal's orders, we start to run.

No time to think any more. Every minute is accounted for, everything we do is under orders, without a moment's rest since this morning. Any form of initiative is inconceivable. We've learned how to fold the sheets and blankets properly (60 by 40cm). Beforehand, you have to shake the blankets really hard, and a great cloud of dust comes off them. I think they must dunk them in a bath of dust before each session. The asthmatics are lucky: they don't have to do it. As from tomorrow, we'll have at least one inspection a day. The lists of duties have been handed out: kitchen, sanitation block, night guard duties. Because we don't have our weapons yet and we haven't learned to shoot, we stand guard round our tents . . . Not exactly useful, because there are other people ensuring the base is secure. But it seems to me that the words 'useful' and 'logical' don't have any tangible meaning. We follow our lessons and are given a hard life. Full stop.

Even so, I feel good. The girls are very cheerful, we laugh the minute we're alone (which is very rarely). No one really knew anyone else before. It's virgin territory. We're having our first adult experience (apparently) together. That forges links quickly.

21st September, midnight

I should really be sleeping. But I've just finished my guard duty. It's very funny. We have to ask for the password – today it's 'coffee without sugar' – from everyone who comes into the tent area. I'm the legionnaire Valerix! If I had any magic potion I'd nip to the kitchens to give the cooks a few ideas. To be honest, the meals are disgusting. I've joined the club of yoghurt eaters. It's good for the figure, but the lack of sleep and the exercises make you so hungry. Luckily, we've got our supplies of biscuits, which we've pooled together.

22nd September, 11.15 p.m.
I'm writing by the light of my watch. Some girls are moaning in their sleep. Keren's sucking her thumb.

We got our guns today. Uzi military pistols. It's terrifying: we incur seven years in prison if they get lost or stolen. We have to keep them on us the whole time, or leave them padlocked to our beds (and what if someone steals the bed?). For now, we've learned the standard warnings. If someone comes near us when we're on guard duty, we have to ask them the password. If they don't answer, we have to say 'Stop!' in a good loud voice, then 'Stop or I'll shoot! Stop or I'll shoot!' (twice). If the person keeps on coming: fire at their legs. If they still keep coming: shoot to kill.

Shoot to kill. They're just words but, strung together, they sound off like an explosion. They can't help it.

That's it, now I can't sleep.

23rd September, 9 a.m.
WE'RE GETTING OUT! 'Habaïta! Habaïta!', that wonderful word which means 'going home'! We're waiting for a bus which is going to take us to the main bus station in Hadera. From there, we're free to go home. And free in every sense of the word until midday on Sunday.

We've waited two hours for the bus. We've been given our permission slips to leave the base. (I can't wait for my permission slips to make phone calls, to flirt, to cry, to see my friends, to do my hair, to read, to write, to put make-up on, to get married, and I don't know what else!)

Hitchhiking is forbidden. Astonishment all round. The roads all over the country are swarming with soldiers holding out their arms and sticking up their thumbs. What are they doing? Some Zen gymnastic exercise, breathing in exhaust fumes?

'That's just the way it is, hitchhiking is forbidden.'

We also have to keep quiet about the name of our base, the names of our officers, non-commissioned officers, fellow soldiers, about how many of us there are, our military numbers . . .

'But the whole country knows about this base,' one girl dared to say. 'Half the country's been through the place!'

'You still can't say anything. In the army, everything is classified as confidential. And anything that isn't confidential is secret.'

'And what isn't secret?'

'Top secret.'

The corporals always have an answer to everything. They've mastered the rules of a game which we'll take a long time to work out.

Two years?

'Everyone back at the base on Sunday. There'll be a bus waiting for you at the bus station in Hadera at eleven o'clock to bring you back here. Be outside your tents at midday. Have a good weekend.'

Some of the girls in my company go part of the way with me, as far as Tel Aviv. We proudly show off our brand new identity papers (soldiers are entitled to free public transport). We expect some sort of reaction from the driver, a smile, a compliment. But he looks grumpy and is profoundly indifferent to our little khaki group. On the other hand, the other passengers all get that adoring expression . . . and it's from looking at us. The people on the street consecrate us as soldiers.

In the bus crossing the Negev towards Beersheva: earphones on. Alone and free. In an hour I'll be back with my family. For now I've got a feeling of absolute freedom. Maybe it's because of the music and the countryside flitting past and the bus forging on. I think I'm beginning to discover that freedom is a movement. And I take great big deep breaths.

It's nearly four o'clock when I finally reach my town, which is already quiet. Winding down for the Sabbath: it's Friday evening and the day of rest is about to start. I feel a bit awkward turning up here in uniform. I suddenly feel as if I'm in fancy dress. Everyone's going to look at me and smile, or laugh. They know Valérie, not private soldier number 3810159.

But I don't meet anyone. Cries of joy echo round when I knock on the door. I didn't have time to let my parents know. Mum's already hugging me to her, Dad's tussling to have his share of me.

'I was sure you'd come out this weekend, I told your father! I've made all your favourite things.'

'Let's have a look at you! You look beautiful, your uniform really suits you!'

'Put your cap on! It's incredible, you really are a soldier!'

I put my cap on. I even salute. They're right: I really am a soldier, and 'it's incredible'. Now that I'm home, with my parents, I can't really work out what that means any more. Nothing's changed, I'm in familiar surroundings, I've only been gone four days. I feel slightly ill at ease, and I can't explain why, but I hide it from them.

For now, I'm the traveller who's returned from an unexplored land. They're firing questions at me.

'Where do you sleep?' Mum asks anxiously.

'In tents.'

'My God! Do you have enough blankets?'

'Of course we do. Anyway, when you're tired you don't feel the cold, you know.'

'And the food?' asks Dad.

'Disgusting.'

He's upset. By my unambivalent reply or by the situation itself. I take the opportunity of the momentary pause to ask where my sister is. They're really sorry: she didn't get leave this week. She'll definitely be out the following weekend. I tell myself that, at this rate, I won't see her for a year. I try to tell them everything, in every detail, but I forget bits and I backtrack to the first day. To the moment I left them.

It's not easy. I'm talking to them about an alien world. Dad tries to draw a few parallels with his military service, during the Algerian war of independence. Mum brushes him aside.

'You've already told us all that a hundred times, that's old news. And, anyway, it's not the same for her: she's a *girl* soldier.'

I can hear all the pride in her words, in the fact that I'm a girl and a soldier. It's comforting.

Having been there for what I reckon is a decent amount of time, I slip away, promising to be home in time for supper. Destination: Rahel and Yulia.

It goes without saying I haven't taken off my uniform.

They welcome me with exclamations which warm my heart.

'Hey, look at the pretty soldier girl!'

'The uniform really, really suits you,' says Yulia. 'I've always said khaki suited brunettes.'

'It goes well with auburn hair too, you know,' I reply in the egalitarian, conciliatory tone that comes naturally to me, or I think it does.

'Put your cap on. We've got to take a photo!'

Rahel goes to get her camera. Click. Then Yulia tries the cap on, and puts on this incredibly languorous expression, like she's a direct descendant of Marilyn Monroe. I've never known how she makes that face. The only time I ever tried, in front of a mirror, I looked like a completely spaced Doberman that hadn't slept for ten days.

Urged on by their questions, I start to tell them about everything. I describe the first day in detail. I tell them about Eynat (who they don't seem very interested in), about Lieutenant Inbar Katz who's so beautiful that we all want to obey her blindly. ('That's rubbish,' mutters Yulia. 'You just obey her because she's your lieutenant.') I tell them about the tents, the blankets dunked in dust, the feeling of being in a holiday camp when we get a few minutes' freedom, the routine and the rest of the time. Marching in time, running, making our beds, learning the first principles, which will soon be followed by others . . .

I can feel their interest waning. So I ask them, 'And what have you been up to in the last four days?'

They've been to the cinema, and to the seaside for a day. They've been shopping in Tel Aviv. One evening they went out with the whole group to a new bar in town called the Orgasma. (For a while now, bar owners have been competing to come up with the hardest name. We've already been treated to Apocalypse Now, Purple Rain, Smashed, The Damned, Dracula . . .)

And they did nothing much: they hung about, together.

We go our separate ways having agreed to go out this evening, like every Friday evening.

I was back at home quite quickly. Mum looked amazed to see me again so soon, but she didn't say anything. While I waited for supper I wrote my diary for a bit, but I didn't manage to establish whether there was a guilty 'camp'. Yulia? Rahel? Me? Who no longer understood who? Who didn't feel like listening to the little details that didn't directly involve them? What had happened, in four days, which meant that our happiness at seeing each other melted away slightly as we actually met up again?

I didn't get anywhere trying to understand the awkwardness. I was sad, but not enough to want to cry about it . . . or to want to talk about it.

The weekend paper with all its supplements was lying on the table. I read Yonatan Geffen's column – I wouldn't miss it for the world. He's unfailingly left-wing, unfailingly corrosive. He criticises the government, the occupation of Palestinian territories, the Israelis' legendary ability to argue without listening to a word anyone else is saying. He's in London at the moment, and he tells us what Israel looks like from there. A tiny little state that no one ever stops talking about. His article helped me breathe a bit more freely. I flicked through the paper, looking for something else. But I wasn't interested in anything that had happened in the world.

I switched the TV on. The news had just started. Riots in the territories, at Jenin. Violence with blazing car tyres, violence with catapults and stones, and violence from our opposing troops, firing rubber bullets. Fifteen Palestinians injured. Three Israelis injured. No deaths today to weigh down one or other of the tallies, to reinforce the hatred or the arguments on either side.

The bus I caught in Hadera to get to Tel Aviv passed just a few kilometres from Jenin. At that point I was probably singing with Tamar, Shlomit and Galit. Perhaps it was even Shlomo Artzi's song 'A New Land'.

We went to a bar that evening and I was pleased to see the boys again, especially Freddy. He talked to me about the base as if he were there, it made me feel like I belonged again.

Dressed in 'civvies' and in among the whole group, all there together, I felt as if nothing had changed, that it was just another Friday evening, and not 48 hours' leave granted to a soldier in D Company of Regiment 3.

I was tired, and I'd had a bit to drink too, but I tossed and turned in my bed for a long time. So I got up and carried out a razzia* in the fridge: some chicken, meatballs hardened by the cold, some gherkins and honey-flavoured semolina cake which Mum made better than anyone else.

It was the first time I'd gorged myself like that with the fridge open and the light off, like a thief.

Saturday sprawled itself between a game of tennis with Mum, some rather empty conversations with Rahel and Yulia, and a great film on TV.

I kept telling myself I should be making more of my leave, that I didn't know when I'd next be at home. But I didn't know what to do: what was there to do except for the usual limited possibilities of a Saturday (a public holiday) in Beersheva, a quiet town (too quiet) in the middle of the desert.

Suddenly I missed Jean-David as much as I had the first day he left. I dialled his number in Jerusalem; after ten rings he picked up and mumbled 'hello' in a very sleepy voice.

I hung up.

Then, I couldn't wait to get back to the base, to be back with my jibing, giggling fellow soldiers who don't know any

* A hostile raid intended for plundering.

of my problems. I couldn't wait to be there, to be the first to launch herself into the intensive training we'd been promised.

I wanted to know what was coming next, because that was going to be my life from now on. But Beersheva, home, my friends, my broken heart which I trailed round with me like a child's blanket . . . from now on they would just be little asides.

PROHIBITED TO UNDER-18s

25th September, 9.30 p.m.
I got back to the base late. I explained that I lived in the
south, that it was 200km with several changes of bus. I'd
discovered that on Sundays the whole country's like a huge
military base with soldiers dashing in every direction,
leaping on buses.

Lieutenant Inbar Katz listened and then said, 'Right, we'll
see whether there are grounds for punishment.'

The girls looked like they really pitied me. I lose the plot
a bit.

I was really glad to see Eynat again. She told me about
the weekend she'd had here. She'd made friends with
half the base but says that I'm the best – she's great! I
was also reunited (but with much less enthusiasm) with
grilled corned beef, served this evening with glutinous
pasta. It's cold and we've been given sleeping bags.

We have to get up at 3.45 a.m. tomorrow.

I'm happy to be here. (Masochist?)

We have to deal with at least 236 events a day, all meticulously timetabled, without a second to breathe. You can't help feeling you're anything but a soldier. There's a new Valérie now, she hardly does any thinking during the day and has definitely given up on the idea of reading her book over the next few weeks. I feel as if I'm making contact with the other Valérie again in the evenings, when I put my earphones on before I go to sleep.

I haven't been punished for getting back late, and I don't think I will be.

I've been on kitchen duties. Like a Lilliputian among giants, cooking pots one metre across, enormous saucepans. We make omelettes using a hundred eggs. For a minute I thought I was in an ogre's kitchen and that I was going to have to make a meal for him, carefully, in fear and devotion, so as not to risk being eaten alive.

I had to wash two hundred plates. Mum couldn't believe it. (I did what everyone does: I woke at two in the morning to phone home. There were 'only' five girls queuing. Mum said she happened to be awake because she was thirsty: I was grateful for the lie.)

Today an officer who deals with postings handed out a list of the different posts available to us. I have the choice between:

The intelligence service

Instructor for fighting soldiers

Officer (In which unit? To do what? Who knows . . .)

Tank technician

Human resources manager

The second appeals most, the fourth too. They strike me as being clear-cut, concrete roles. And I'd love to command soldiers, obviously. But the dice are loaded. I sat a lot of exams for the intelligence service before I signed up. They create this illusion that I can choose. I could always create the illusion that I believe it, just for a few more days.

We've had our first weapons lesson. We learned how to strip down and reassemble a machine gun in less than three minutes. Why do you need to know how to strip down your weapon? To clean it, forsooth! With this thick black oil which smells of rubber, and a cloth with a pretty little name: 'flanelite'. We make a proud sight, crouching in the sun pulling our guns to pieces.

We've also had a military history lesson, with a screening of a very moving film about the war of independence*. A 23-year-old captain was fighting an amazing battle in the mountains above Jerusalem. (I don't know why I said 'amazing battle', it was the captain who was amazing.) At the end of the documentary, they explained the strategic importance of what we'd just seen, and they told us the captain had died off camera. We felt really sad.

---

* In 1948.

We were asked to give blood for injured soldiers. It wasn't compulsory but I went along. Because of the film, I'm pretty sure.

They didn't want my blood: my blood pressure was too low.

Tomorrow we're going to start running with our equipment.

29th September, 8 p.m.

Exhausted. But I'm discovering resources of physical resistance I would never have guessed I had. It's as if someone's pushing me the whole time, ordering me to get up the minute I threaten to drop. This morning: exercises first thing, then MAJOR clear-up for MAJOR inspection. In other words, an inspection carried out by Lieutenant Inbar Katz and not by our corporal, Kineret. In honour of what? We don't know. To fill up our timetable, probably.

It was too much of an ordeal. We had to start all over again four times. The first time, one blanket hadn't had all the dust shaken off it. We had to shake all of them all over again. The second time, a girl in one of the other tents burst out laughing when she was standing to attention. The third time, Vered, in our tent, had left her brush on her bed. HER BRUSH ON HER BED! We were gobsmacked by such a lapse. We threatened to shave her head if she re-offended, and she went and cried. The fourth time, the tent hadn't been swept well enough, you could still see footprints.

Then it was our first big run. The whole shebang: the

bullet-proof vest, the Uzi submachine gun, two loaders and a full water bottle. Plus three-litre cans of water (which, inevitably, weighed three kilos) which we carried in relays. We ran round a field of maize, right next to the base. For the first few minutes we really felt fascinating, like 'Rambo girls'. Then the group morphed into a bedraggled column: the sporty ones at the front looking graceful and light-footed despite the equipment, and the flabby, the weak and the lazy at the back. I was pretty much between the two. Not light-footed and gracious, but sweating, short of breath, my face probably distorted by the strain and by my fierce desire not to be among the last.

The hardest part was not having a shower when we got back. We wash in the evenings. And tough luck if there are some none-too-subtle smells.

This afternoon a lesson on shooting in the prone position. Every time I handle my weapon, I feel as if I'm two people at the same time – it's really disturbing. When I fill my loader, I warm the bullets with my hands. The Uzi bullets are a 9mm calibre. They're rounded at the tip and they're quite dumpy compared to the 7.75mm bullets in an M16 which are long, pointed . . . and terrifying. I didn't know bullets could have a personality.

To end the day on a beautiful note, we started learning how to march in formation for parades.

And, now it's all over, I feel like I've got precious little left in my brain, I can't even think. I'm beginning to miss having time on my own.

Friday 30ᵗʰ September, 4.20 p.m.

We're staying at the base this weekend. I rang home and Mum told me that I'd passed my bac with an A–! I was only just short of the A grade, because of the maths (or rather because of Jean-David). But that all seems such a long time ago . . . what does the bac mean in this place?

The day's shorter today, and tomorrow we won't do much, apart from kitchen duty and guard duty. In the army they respect the day of rest too. And, I have to say, I'm going to make a point of respecting it right now.

Time for sleep.

Saturday 1ˢᵗ October, 4.30 p.m.

Today's a strange day: there's this new feeling of being soldiers but with nothing to do, just soldiers, just at the base, without the excitement, the exhaustion, the despair (sometimes) of the previous few days. We were treated to a special meal: rubbery chicken, greasy potatoes (but they were pretty good, it has to be said) and treacly wine. We're making the most of our spare time and exploring the base.

I took a little path which leads from our tent: it ended up in a small wood of eucalyptus trees. The eucalyptus is a special tree, I thought to myself. It's very big but not at all oppressive, perhaps because it's so light. And it has such a serious name, it doesn't have a common name like most trees and plants. The smell of them reminded me of childhood colds; Mum always used to put a few drops of eucalyptus oil on my pillow to help me breathe. I also know that here in Israel it was the pioneers who planted them at the turn of the twentieth century, to dry out swampy areas of land and contain malaria epidemics. Were eucalyptus trees planted in Tsahal bases for their therapeutic properties? I think it's more likely that their tall screen of foliage keeps prying eyes from military secrets . . . us, in this instance.

Behind the eucalyptus trees are the barbed wire fences. They startle me a bit – I wasn't expecting them, not here, in the middle of my reminiscing and my botanical ramblings. To me the very words 'barbed wire' rip your skin. I go up to it carefully. There's a freshly ploughed field right there, less than a metre away. Further away there's a road that I can't see very clearly because the ground isn't level. There are cars passing: people going to the seaside, or for picnics – it's a nice day today. I can picture them, I piece them together, like an over-laden memory trying to remember something which once existed, but which is no longer there.

When I went back to the tent, the girls said I looked weird. I didn't feel like explaining. Luckily, most of them have enough energy and vitality to cope with anything. We sang songs, then we had fun inventing slogans. I should say that the base is dotted with big billboards with signs like:

Soldiers, drive carefully! Better five minutes late in this world than five decades early in the next!

Soldiers, make sure your uniform is always spotless! A correctly dressed soldier is an efficient soldier in combat!

Soldiers, salute anyone higher ranking than yourself. Respect for your seniors opens the way for order.

I made them laugh by saying that they're like Chinese

philosophical sayings. Galit started bellowing, 'Soldiers, sol-
diers, soldiers! Where are the soldiers, there are only girls
here, where are the soldiers, that's what I came for!'

So we invented this one:

Soldier girls, find the soldier of your dreams! Love will give
you some respite!

So basically we mucked about, and it was very relaxing.

Kineret came to spend some time with us. As soon as we
saw her we leapt into square formation, standing to attention. She smiled and said, 'Hey, no, girls, it's a rest day today.
I just came by to see how it was going.'

She sat down with us. Galit, Riki and Sivan (who are the
most talkative, or maybe the most confident) started asking
her questions.

'Where are you from?'

'From a kibbutz in Galilee.'

'Which one?'

'Kfar Blum.'

'You lucky thing! Did you go kayaking every day?'

'Not every day, but quite often.'

'Have you been here long?'

'How old are you?'

I felt like I was back at school when we wanted to know
everything about our teachers (single? Married? Any children? A house or an apartment? Any dogs? A piano?).

Kineret didn't let us swamp her. She shook her hair and
said, 'Hang on, I want to get to know you too. Can I ask you
the same questions back?'

We didn't find it so interesting talking about ourselves, so we tried to steer the conversation towards the army, towards what lay ahead for us here over the next few weeks.

'When are we going to fire guns for real?'

'What's the furthest we'll have to run?'

'Are there any boys in this base, or none at all, apart from the fat cook?'

'When will we know which units we're being posted to?'

Kineret answered some of the questions, but not all of them. It didn't matter that we were chatting like a bunch of friends who'd gone off on holiday together, it didn't matter that she was nineteen at the oldest (you're made a corporal in the fourth month of military service, and you stay at that rank for eighteen months before becoming a sergeant – the maths is simple), she was still our instructor and she too must have been given explicit instructions on exactly how much we could get to know about her.

She got up with a 'Make the most of your free time: tomorrow it's back to the routine.'

2nd October, 9.15 p.m.

A five-kilometre run this morning. Apparently our last run will be fifteen! I'll probably be dead before then, or transformed into an air-conditioning device, puffing and puffing . . .

Shooting lesson, too. When you're shooting lying down you rest your cheek against the butt, and there's something so gentle about that movement. Then the automatic firing position, standing with the gun against your hip.

Why should I hide the fact? I'm fascinated by my sub-machine gun. They're instruments of death and we're finding them easier and easier to handle. We don't think for a moment that we might use them for real some day. But at the same time it's the ultimate sign that we really are soldiers, on completely equal terms with the boys. And it makes me feel proud when I think about it.

We had a test to assess our abilities to take command. It was a sort of role play and we had to explain the point of military service to the company, then to deal with those who wouldn't accept the military logic. I think I didn't do too badly.

To finish off: a first aid lesson with a mega-realistic film illustrating the sort of wounds you get from conventional bullets, exploding bullets, mortars, various burns and chemical and biological weapons. Then we had explanations of tourniquets, injections, antidotes, bandaging and comforting words we should use. They reiterated that Israeli soldiers never abandon a dead or wounded soldier on enemy ground. Even at the risk of other human lives.

Tomorrow I'm head of company.

4th October, 9 p.m.

Yesterday evening after supper we had a really moving conversation with Kineret. Subject: what exactly is the link that connects us to Israel, this country which has only been going since 1948 and which is full of Jews from all over the world? Some said it was the land of our ancestors: Abraham, Isaac, Jacob and David. Others felt that the extermination of the

European Jews during the Second World War had proved that there was a need for a Jewish state where they could take refuge if they were threatened. A few girls whose reasoning was basically pretty sound said that they'd been born here and that usually people were attached to their native country. Then Kineret read us two texts which I've copied out here:

A Fly on the Wall in New Zealand
By Adi Lewinson

I sometimes wonder what it feels like to live in New Zealand. Travelling through the Pacific islands, living in a country that's difficult to find on maps, growing up in a town with red roofs and taking walks in the green countryside, living in a house built by an ancestor, being the grandson of a grandfather who died of old age, studying two hundred years' worth of history in a slim grey book, getting wine from the barrel in the cellar. A cellar which doesn't serve as a shelter.

Being a New Zealander and making five-year plans, getting worked up about the exploits of the local football team, maybe signing up for a career in the army, given that there is no compulsory military service. Being free of the army, with the hope of living 'an exciting life', reading a New Zealand newspaper and not understanding what's going on in the Holy Land, why people fight over every scrap of land when the world is such a big place and life is so precious. Believing that all men are equal.

Being a New Zealander and knowing that cannons are fired only on the queen's birthday, that a bullet is a high-speed train in Japan, that a sleeping bag is something you use when you're camping, and that a widow is usually an old woman. And when the neighbour says her son has fallen, asking whether he hurt himself.

I'm not reproaching you, God, for having chosen our nation for this. I accept this sentence with love and pride. I wouldn't swap Jerusalem for Wellington, or my life here for an easier one anywhere else in the world. This is my land!

But is it true that in New Zealand people die of boredom?

She was born in Sweden

She was born in Sweden,
Golden hair and children who don't play war games,
Innocents who don't ask if God exists
because they don't need him.
And me here,
a quiet little piece of land
which history has turned into a knot of tensions
with endless complications.
Youths in the prime of their lives
are heroes here, every day.
And they don't ask if God exists
because they're afraid of the answer.
She came to see us,
a place she'd been told was a homeland.
We met in the summer holidays,
we dreamed that everything was possible.
After two months, once she'd seen everything,
once she'd loved,

once she'd had her fill of my homeland she went back
                                                      there,
to her wonderfully peaceful existence.
In her letters she sometimes tells me how much she
                                                  loves me,
and asks me to join her, to be with her for ever.
She has a house beside the sea.
Back there, in Sweden, like in children's stories.
Personally, I think she's right.
But one rainy night I stayed awake for hours,
and I wrote to tell her I loved her.
I couldn't explain to her or to myself
that I owed someone three years of my life,
and then my whole life.
And may Massada* not fall a second time.

When Kineret spoke the famous incantation And may Massada not fall a second time in her gentle voice, we were all in tears, ready to take up arms and see ourselves wiped out on the spot to protect our little country. This country where there are widows of thirty, where the cannons have never fallen silent and where, when someone says their neighbour's son has 'fallen', everyone knows that it's in the war. In an emotional silence, each of us was thinking that

* A fortress overlooking the Dead Sea. In the first century AD a few hundred Jews resisted for many months as a powerful Roman army laid siege to them. Having exhausted their supplies, they decided to commit suicide – men, women and children. Zionist epics resuscitated this heroic (but not unique) episode in Jewish resistance to the Roman occupation, and made it a national symbol.

she was part of a great heavy chain of history, a chain of deaths but also of hope. All except one of us. Daniela (from the other tent) said rather haughtily, 'That's completely stupid. That's called propaganda.'

Kineret raised an eyebrow, and the other girls pretty much threw themselves at her, shouting, 'You don't know what you're saying! It's our country we're talking about! Our history! You have no right to say that!'

Daniela stayed calm and just replied, 'You swallow everything that's served up for you. They tell you about this idyllic country and you just believe in it naively. Those syrupy words are fine on TV on Independence Day. They're fine for getting crowds to believe that we're so beautiful, aren't they? So kind, so sensitive, such pacifists, but that, UNFORTUNATELY, we're always having to defend ourselves.'

'But that's the truth,' Vered protested.

'What truth? The truth you want to believe in, so that you don't have to ask yourself any questions about the uniform we're wearing, about what it means to the Palestinians, for example.'

There was a short silence. I don't think anyone had specifically thought about that. Kineret was listening to the debate with interest but she still didn't intervene. Emotion took over again.

'That's not true! That's got nothing to do with it! We have a very special history, Jews have been persecuted all over the place for centuries and the Zionist pioneers sacrificed themselves so that we could live here in peace –'

'But it's got a lot "to do with it",' Daniela interrupted. 'So long as we have this romantic, irreproachable image of ourselves, we'll carry on oppressing a people without even realising it.'

'But they're the ones who . . .'

The Palestinian argument floundered on. Once all the points had been put forward, Daniela stood her ground as the 'patriotic camp' threw a few things in her face: the dead in the Holocaust, and those from the war of independence, the Six Days' War, the Yom Kippur War and the war in the Lebanon. And in among the dead there was a grandmother, an uncle, a father, a brother, a cousin, a friend . . .

I didn't say a word: I didn't have anyone close to me to exhume. I also thought that Daniela wasn't altogether wrong, but that you had to say things differently, to explain, without causing so much hurt, without provoking these tears, without calling everything back into question.

Or you really had to despair, to take off your uniform and desert on the spot.

5th October, 8.50 p.m.

We had the fifteen-kilometre run today . . . and I only did seven of it. Is it the pressure of the last few days, being in this monochrome universe for too long, being condemned to thinking for only half an hour of the day (when I'm writing)? It must be. As I ran, I concocted the kind of scam you come up with in primary school: one of the lenses in my glasses has a tendency to drop out. Halfway through the run I discreetly made it fall into my pocket. I called Kineret and told her that I couldn't really see properly. She didn't try and make trouble for me, gave me an exemption note and asked the jeep which was following us to take me back to the base where I would easily get a lift to Hadera.

Four hours on my own! Four hours of total freedom! I had trouble disguising my delight.

In Hadera, which I'd never been to before, I popped the lens back in place and settled on the terrace of the first cafe I could find. I looked around in amazement: people of all ages, dressed in black, white and every other colour, babies in buggies, children scampering around . . . They were the ones I watched with the most curiosity: I hadn't seen children for such a long time. No one normally notices children in the street, but I now live in a world where, although you can meet men and women between 18 and 50, you never see children. I realised that I missed them, or rather that not having them around didn't really seem normal.

I live in a world prohibited to under-18s, I thought to myself.

I did nothing for three whole hours. I didn't write anything, I didn't even ring home or Rahel or Yulia. I quenched my thirst for all the sounds of the town, for the nondescript little houses (which weren't prefabricated) and for people.

I breathed in the intoxicating smell of stolen freedom.

6th October, 9.20 a.m.
We'd pretty much guessed, but the information has just been confirmed by an extremely reliable source: we're getting out this weekend!

...WHERE NO ONE DIES OF BOREDOM

I'm beginning to feel at home on the Egged Company's red buses which criss-cross their way over the country. I've got my little routine: a seat by the window if possible, music in my earphones, looking out at the countryside – so green compared to the Negev. It's the sort of countryside they sing about in those songs about 'Beautiful Israel', the land of the pioneers' descendants: robust, healthy workers with confident, determined expressions and terrible clothes (but they pay so little attention to that sort of thing that no one notices). Their distinguishing characteristic: they like singing together in chorus, in the evenings, round the camp fire – often Russian revolutionary songs which have been translated into Hebrew.

Every time, without fail, I slide down in my seat, rest my legs up against the seat in front, and close my eyes.

They say that driving sends children to sleep . . . and

soldiers too.

I wake up in the middle of the desert, like the last time. I know from a factory on the left that I'll be in Beersheva in a quarter of an hour. It's almost as if that squat grey building plonked in the middle of nowhere is there as a landmark for travellers. How many times in the next two years will that factory tell me that I'm heading back home?

I feel relaxed, or rather as if I'm outside myself, a stranger. Half of me is at the base and half of me is 'at home'. And the two parts will never be joined together again, I'm sure of it. Nothing can unite those two worlds, I'll just have to make my own arrangements to cope with a double life . . . without becoming a schizophrenic.

I once read that some prisoners, once they've done their time, can't really take proper advantage of their newfound freedom. They don't know what to do with it, they're terrified of it, they drown in it and get depressed. That's when they turn back to crime, just to get back to prison.

My sister Sonia isn't at home, and I'm beginning to miss her. My parents make a big show of how happy they are to see me after a fortnight's absence, but they seem a bit awkward, disorientated. They look at me as if I've grown thirty centimetres overnight. Have I changed that much? Me, on the inside, my attitude, or is it the magic of uniform?

You don't talk to a soldier the same way you would to a teenager. No one tells them to tidy their room, to turn the music down or to get off the phone. I will no longer hear those words which punctuated my life with my parents up until just a few weeks ago.

It feels like such a brutal change.

A soldier is a sort of adult with even more responsibilities than her parents. She's carrying the national security on her shoulders. That's what our corporal, Kineret, told us one evening.

I call Rahel and Yulia; I can't wait to see them and to talk to them, even if they don't understand everything.

They're very excited. The countdown's started for them: they've been called up for the 17th of October. They're highly likely to be in the same base as each other and perhaps even the same company. What mysterious mechanism of fate in the army's bureaucracy decided to send me off into combat alone and to put my two best friends together?

Today, perhaps because the fateful day is drawing near for them, they pay much more attention to everything I tell them. To redress the balance in our relationships it's now my turn to be detached, seasoned, even a bit superior in spite of myself. I'm a little way ahead of them in the military world. Just as, last year, I was the first to spend the night with a boy, and for a few months I was in possession of a knowingness they didn't yet have.

Yulia leaves to go and have a deep bubble bath. It's her great weakness. Two years ago we both decided to write down the top one hundred dreams, longings or plans that we wanted to realise in our lives. It makes me smile when I think back to it: one hundred, it's such a childish number . . . One of Yulia's wishes was to have a bath in champagne. She probably got the idea from some article about Madonna or

Elizabeth Taylor, she lives off a daily diet of celebrity magazines.

I said I wanted to meet the man of my life and to have two children. I wanted to write a book, travel to Italy, Spain and New York; and to Auschwitz too. My 25th wish was: still to be Yulia's friend in twenty years' time.

Twenty years, that's the only length of time we can imagine, and even that's quite hard.

We'd planned to tick off the dreams scrupulously as they were realised, and to establish statistics: the number of realisations per annum, displayed on a graph so that you could tell at a glance the good and bad years; the percentage of realisations we each had after five, ten, fifteen and twenty years.

Rahel's silence tears me away from my daydreaming. Something's up.

'Are you OK?' I ask her, making it sound positive.

'OK,' she replies, her throat tight.

'Well, that means you're not,' I say gently, and she doesn't say anything. 'What is it? Are you worried about the army? Don't worry. Once you're there you don't even have time to think. You feel like a robot, you can't help it, but it's not a bad thing, really. And, anyway, you might be with Yulia . . .'

She bites her lip and looks away. I realise I haven't got it at all. I sometimes have a way of throwing myself into other people's sadness and wanting to console them as quickly as possible: too quickly, perhaps. I give her a hug.

'Rahel, what is it?'

She stays stubbornly silent. I know she wants to talk, otherwise she would have found a way of hiding how she was feeling. She's the past master of concealment, our Rahel. But I love her all the more when she shows how vulnerable she is.

A sudden spark of intuition.

'Freddy?'

I get a strangled 'yes' in reply.

Damn! He's leaving her to go back to Inbar, his ex, who he talks about with a bit too much admiration in his voice . . . who he talks about too much, full stop.

To do that to Rahel just before she goes off on her military service! (A nasty little voice in my head whispers: So what? Jean-David dumped you right in the middle of your *bac* – and you got over it, didn't you? – No, that's just it, I don't want to go thinking they're all bastards. Jean-David isn't a bastard, I still love him. And Freddy's my friend.)

'When?' I ask her bracingly, to get her to confide in me finally.

'Tomorrow evening.'

'Tomorrow evening?!' (I don't understand: he's let her know about a post-dated break-up? That's weird, I didn't think he was so . . . calculating.)

'Yes, tomorrow evening. He doesn't want to go on like this. He can't handle it any more. The military police are seriously searching for him at the moment. He's been hiding with Rafi for two weeks, my parents have refused to have him at home. So he's decided to hand himself in, to take his punishment and go back to the army.'

I daren't tell her that I'd thought it was something completely different. Anyway, she's finally burst into tears and

I've taken her in my arms. I tell her I'm there, that we're all there, that we love her, that it had to happen sooner or later, that she'd known for a month that one day he'd give up this stolen freedom. Then I reassure her that he won't suffer, and that – when it comes down to it – I can't see what difference there could be between a 'normal' military base and a prison base. There must be eucalyptus trees there too, and latrine duties, kitchen duties, tents and sleeping bags. I intoxicate her with words of consolation, I feel so close to her when I know she needs me . . .

We stay there on the grass for a long time, talking in a way I thought was no longer possible.

As we say goodbye, I ask, 'Have you got any plans for this evening?'

'We're going to see Stanley Kubrick's *A Clockwork Orange*. Ilan says it's a cult film.'

'What time's everyone leaving?'

'Be ready by about nine.'

'OK. I love you, you know that?'

I give her a kiss, and run back to have the first meal worthy of the name for a fortnight.

Being back with my group of friends puts me in a good mood. Freddy's very talkative, and I whisper in his ear, 'Rahel told me about tomorrow. We'll be here. For her and for you.'

A serious expression flickers across his eyes and he squeezes my hand. It feels like everyone's talking more than usual, getting worked up about nothing in particular. Perhaps trying to outwit the inevitable; definitely doing anything to avoid referring to what's looming tomorrow. At the cinema I sit between Ilan and Rahel, and she's next to Freddy. They're discreet but they're huddled slightly closer together than usual. She seems so fragile next to his large frame.

I suddenly feel sad: at least they love each other. They'll only be separated for a while.

I turn to Ilan, who acts like a big brother to all of us girls, especially when things are difficult.

'How long's the film?'

'Two hours and seventeen minutes exactly.' His eyes are shining. He's been wanting to see *A Clockwork Orange* for a long time, but it's banned to under-16s and isn't screened very frequently.

I yawn. The ads are going on and on. Then the lights go out, a shiver runs through the packed auditorium where the average age is twenty. Some people are asking those in front of them to sit down lower. Others are impatiently telling them to be quiet. I can feel unusual tension. I've never seen any of Stanley Kubrick's films; my cult film is Chaplin's *The Kid*, and his *The Great Dictator* too.

There's a close-up of someone with one eye surrounded by false eyelashes, and wearing a funny black bowler hat. The camera pans out and reveals two other identical men, and naked women being used as tables. They're blow-up dolls . . . I'm beginning to have my doubts about Ilan's taste.

The three men are in a car park, they're laying into an old drunk really violently. Ilan leans towards me. 'It's great, they're speaking in Russian slang.'

I couldn't give a stuff about the Russian, and I'm feeling

really, really terrible. This isn't at all the kind of thing I felt like seeing while I was on leave: violence, however far removed it may be.

Ilan's shoulder is close, really close. I've been up since 3.45 this morning, I would have no trouble at all closing my eyes if I rested my head somewhere.

Half asleep, I hear *I'm singing in the rain* set against background screaming, but it's not Gene Kelly singing. I think I'm having a nightmare, I must be overtired.

There are some evenings when it's not cult films that you need.

I wake in the night to plunder the fridge, and the food tastes strange just because it's cold. I don't really understand this impulse: I'm not hungry, but I have this need to fill my stomach without really enjoying it, really quickly, like there's some gap that just has to be filled.

I've spent some of the day with Rahel. We didn't talk much; we put music on and mostly sang together. Songs are better at talking about life than we are, I told her. What's the point in trying to outdo them?

She and Freddy have agreed to meet at 6 p.m., to spend a bit of time together before we all go to the military police station with him. It's getting dark early: I ask Rahel if she'd like to go down and watch the sunset with me.

The dark, rectangular form of our school (our old school now – already!) is silhouetted against the desert. To the left of it the golden disc is sinking slowly as if about to drown itself in the sand. The sky changes colour with every second. It's such a beautiful sight it takes your breath away. We're huddled together, united by all the sunsets we've watched together, and by the question that neither of us asks: when will the next one be?

With the timings of our respective leaves, we may not see each other for a long time.

'We'll write to each other,' whispers Rahel.

'Yes,' I reply. 'But who'll watch the sun when we're not here?'

Back home, Mum greets me with a twinkle in her eye and asks triumphantly, 'Guess who called you?'

'I dunno.' I'm not exactly dying to play guessing games. She looks a bit disappointed by my reaction but still has that child-in-a-sweetie-shop expression of someone harbouring a wonderful secret.

'Jean-David.'

'WHAT?'

'Actually, it's who, not what! Jean-David rang to speak to you ten minutes ago.'

I close my eyes and let the happiness flood through me. And I smile, like I don't think I've smiled for a very long time.

'He said you could get hold of him till about seven,' Mum adds, still really pleased.

I pounce on the phone and Mum tiptoes out of the living room. My heart's beating so hard: what am I going to say to him? Why's he calling nearly four months after we split up?

It rings once: my hands are shaking. I'm suddenly frightened that I'm too happy, and that in a few seconds I'll be falling back down from a great height.

It rings twice. If he hasn't answered by the fourth ring, I'll hang up.

It rings a third time.

'Hello?'

His voice, the register of it, the familiar note of irony I think I can detect (but I'm probably wrong).

'It's Valérie.' (My voice is breathy, trying so hard to be relaxed.)

'What a surprise!' he exclaims in Hebrew, but getting it slightly wrong.

'You don't say it like that,' I say, suddenly bolstered by my undeniable superiority over him in a language he's only been crucifying for a few months. 'And, anyway, it's not a surprise – you called me.'

'*Ken, ken, at tsodeket*,*' he says in an earthy voice which he thinks is an Israeli accent. He's clowning around. There's one of two explanations: he's not on his own, or he doesn't know what to say. It's not looking good.

'How are things?' he asks.

I feel like slapping him, so I reply with disproportionate enthusiasm.

'Perfect. I'm having the most fantastic holiday up in the north. It's so wonderful that I get up at half past three every morning to be sure I don't miss anything. It's a four-star

* Yes, yes, you're right.

resort with all the mod cons, sand beneath your feet, showers just across the way and temperatures that drop to ten below at night. Do you want the address?'

I get silence in reply. I realise I've never spoken to him so freely, without considering every word, without wanting to seem intelligent more than anything else. I get the feeling I've scored a point. (But what sort of match are we playing?)

His voice softens. 'Listen, I've been thinking about you, really. I imagine it's . . . no, I don't actually imagine anything. I'd like you to tell me about it. Maybe you could make a detour to Jerusalem between two postings?'

A detour to Jerusalem! I'd see his laughing eyes again, his hands! I'd kiss him, even if it's only on the cheek. I want to tell him I'm coming, right away, that – funnily enough – I have to go to Jerusalem for military reasons (it's a bit crass, but what the hell, he's got no way of checking). I feel like I've got wings, nothing can hold me back.

Or can it?

Freddy's handing himself in this evening, and Rahel needs me.

So I say yes, I think I can go via Jerusalem, maybe in a week's time, when my course is over but before the beginning of whatever's coming next, a course at another base, probably. We chat for a few more minutes; my heart has calmed down and I hang up with the promise that I'll give him some sign of life very soon.

The questions are milling round my head. I ring Yulia, and tell her the news with barbaric whoops of joy into the receiver. 'I'm on my way!' she says, and here she is in my room already, making me go over and over the conversation word for word, his tone of voice, mine when I spoke to him . . . She's our relationship analysis expert, she reads everything on the subject that she can get her hands on, and she's accumulated a fair few TV series from which she's drawn valuable information.

After an hour, she gives her verdict.

'He's bound to want to see you in uniform. It's a very common fantasy with Europeans and Americans. You have to go, and to find out straightaway what the score is with him. But don't get your hopes up, it might just be what he felt like at the time . . .'

Now that's a sentence she'd have done better to have kept to herself.

Ilan rings me.

'We're all meeting up outside Rahel's in ten minutes.'

I put on my uniform, in the hope that having a soldier who's completely above board around might soften our friend's fate.

There are about fifteen of us, split between three cars. Rafi's arguing with Rahel: he doesn't want her to drive (he doesn't say 'in that state' but he might as well have done), and she's obstinately refusing to let anyone else take the wheel. I gesture discreetly to Rafi and he gives up trying to persuade her.

Freddy puts on a sad song about John Lennon's death.

There are tears rolling slowly down my cheeks. I think Rahel is driving with tears in her eyes.

The military police station is plonked at the end of a dusty drive, in a sort of no-man's-land. The soldier on duty by the door looks perplexed by our group. Perhaps he's wondering whether he should fire a shot in the air. We stop a few metres short of the steps, a compact, nervous little flock. Freddy steps forward with Rahel leaning in close to him.

'I'm a deserter,' he says in a serious voice, 'and I've come to hand myself in.'

The soldier shows no particular emotion.

'Give me your papers,' he orders him, 'and follow me.'

We all look down so as not to watch the moment of separation. Someone mumbles, 'See you, Freddy!' and we all join in in chorus, 'See you, Freddy. See you soon.'

The soldier doesn't deign to look at us. Freddy disappears without looking back and we stand there motionless. There's nothing more to do, but we can't leave so soon.

The silence is unbearable.

Rahel's gone bright red. She's going to explode. I go over to her and whisper, 'Race you back to the cars?'

On the way home, I think back to that piece about New Zealand that Kineret read to us. I tell myself we're only eighteen and, as we say in Hebrew, all this is too big for us.

FIRE!

9th October, 9.45 p.m.

Not that easy going back to being number 3810159 after all the emotion of the weekend. I'd give ten years of my life for a few days' freedom straightaway. To be with Rahel, to comfort her as best I can, but specially – why should I lie about it – to take the next bus to Jerusalem. But none of that's possible, I'm here till Friday and then I'll be answer- able to another group of officers and corporals. An invisible hand has already chosen my posting and decided my life. Is that what it means to be an adult?

Last weapons lesson this afternoon, before the big day – tomorrow – when we fire real bullets for the first time.

Intensive training this morning: two hours running round the base, tackling the climbing wall, scrambling under nets, all probably to get us into shape for the day of reckoning.

Then a gathering of all the troops with Inbar Katz (looking sexier than ever), who gives us these instructions:

'Soldiers, at the shooting range, it is absolutely ESSENTIAL that you scrupulously respect every order. It's no longer a question of hierarchy, it's a question of life and death. Negligence, poor concentration and silly mistakes can cause irreversible disasters. You must get it into your heads that you're not only responsible for yourselves, but for the others too.'

There's something alarming in her tone of voice, a seriousness which says, 'Watch out, now! This isn't a game. You're not performing in some Oscar-winning film, or even a B-movie.' She uttered the words life and death, and they've suddenly taken on a peculiar consistency, they now hang on a chubby little 9mm-calibre bullet. The excitement we were feeling a few minutes before has dissipated.

That's clearly what she was hoping to achieve.

We climb into troop transport lorries exactly like the ones we often see making their way to the Lebanese border. Silence reigns – it's impossible to speak anyway because we're thrown about unceremoniously by the most unbelievable jolts. We're in danger of dying in a road accident before we fire our first bullets.

The shooting range: sand, pebbles, cardboard targets of human silhouettes about the size of an average man.

We're going to fire in groups of ten – each company is divided into two. The soldiers who aren't shooting have to stay within a security perimeter. Anyone who leaves it without permission is liable to a month's imprisonment.

I catch sight of Eynat who's giving me an encouraging little wave. She's among the first to fire and she's heading off with a smile.

I sit slightly apart from the others. The sun's burning and the bullet-proof vest is making me hot. I can hear the shots, but I'm not watching the girls shooting.

The instructions we've been given for shooting a 'suspect' who turns out to be an 'enemy' come back to me: the last sentence is *'shoot to kill'*. I hear those words and they become the voice-over for a report on the territories that I saw on TV on Saturday, just the same as the one I saw a fortnight before. Well, nearly the same: the images were identical (stones hurled from catapults, burning car tyres, tear gas, shots) but it wasn't the same men dying.

Girl soldiers are not sent into combat in the territories. Girl soldiers don't go into combat.

What sense can I make of this shooting session today, of these targets I can't bring myself to look at, even if they are in cardboard? Tears are now mingling with the sweat trickling down my forehead. Someone puts their hand on my shoulder. Kineret's smiling at me.

'Are you feeling all right?'

'Not really.'

'Are you frightened of shooting?'

'It's not really that I'm frightened . . . I'm just thinking about the implications.'

She sits down next to me.

'What implications?'

'It's complicated. I was thinking how I'd react if one day I really had to shoot, to shoot a person, in flesh and blood. I'm also wondering which side I'm on. I wish I could avoid choosing one camp or another.'

'What do you mean a camp?'

'You know what I mean,' I mutter, 'stones or guns.'

She takes a deep breath and says, 'I asked myself the same questions when I shot for the first time, right here, a few months ago. The Intifada helped me find the answers. Do you know what Tsahal actually means?'

'Of course I do: it's the initial letters of the Israeli defence army.'

'Exactly. Now, that's what you've got to remember: *defence* army. You'll never have to use your weapon against someone unless that someone is threatening your life. You'd have to defend yourself then, to protect yourself and to protect others.'

'But why would I have an enemy who'd want to kill me ?'

'Don't hide behind that disingenuous attitude. Obviously the minute you put on a uniform you're no longer an individual as far as other people are concerned. You represent the Israeli army, the one that confronts the Palestinians every day . . . whatever your own feelings and convictions may be. That's the way it is, but it shouldn't stop you thinking.'

I'm still perplexed. She gets up and pats me on the shoulder.

'Don't worry. Everything will be fine.'

They're calling numbers from D Company at the moment. We're lined up in front of a row of sand bags, with our guns slung from shoulder to waist. We're being handed earphones to prevent our eardrums bursting with the explosions. Inbar Katz is at the end of the line, to my right.

'Soldiers, from now on you will carry out my orders accurately and immediately . . . take the straps off your weapons.'

We do as we're told, hearts thumping.

'Assume the prone position.

'Put the loader into your weapons, keeping the barrel aimed at the target. Do not put your fingers on the trigger.

'Aim at the target. Remove the safety catch. Line your weapon up along the line of fire. Now, be ready, but you must wait for the order to fire for each of the five bullets.

'On my order . . . ready . . . FIRE!'

There's a moment's hesitation after her order, then a few timid shots (if such a powerful shot can be timid) ring out. I concentrate, clamp my gun to my shoulder and my cheek to avoid being injured by the kick. I fire.

'FIRE!'

A second shot. You can't think about anything else when you're shooting, it's the only thing you can think about.

'FIRE!'

A third shot, which must have come close to the target's heart.

'FIRE!'

A fourth shot. I think my aim's getting better and better.

'FIRE!'

The cartridge falls to the ground just below my nose. Fifth and final bullet. Already.

'Keep the barrel pointing towards the target. Remove your loaders. Check that they're empty. Put the safety catch back on. Don't move.

'Corporal Kineret!'

'Yes, ma'am.'

'Go through the ranks of the whole company, count the cartridges and check the loaders.'

I haven't moved a muscle, I'm still looking dead ahead, but I'm convinced Kineret smiled at me as she picked up my cartridges.

'Soldiers, lay down your arms. Corporal Kineret, carry out the target check.'

Kineret gives us our results: I put two bullets into the target's heart, the others just beside it. Apparently that's really very good for a first effort from twenty-five metres.

11th October, 6 p.m.
The shooting session yesterday: torn between pride and consternation. The timetable's gone a bit topsy-turvy this evening: we're on duty, for real. In my case, from midnight till two a.m. in a strategic place – the armoury. The password today is 'full moon'. Some people just can't help being poetic.

12th October, 2.30 a.m.
It was strange: the night seemed darker than usual, and more mysterious or threatening. I was with a girl from

another tent who seemed to frighten pretty easily. It wasn't hard for me to get contaminated by her fear. Every rustle of foliage, every cricket that little bit noisier than the others seemed suspect. Like when you're young and you spend the night at home alone for the first time.

At one point the noises really did get worrying: it sounded like someone was sneaking along very close to us. We started saying the set words of warning, terrified by the sound of our own voices. I wasn't sure whether to fire in the air. I switched my torch on and it lit up a pile of wood right next to us. A family of rats was playing happily between the planks! We screamed in disgust and were still terrified when the relief guards arrived.

Kineret came by to see us, and she teased us gently.

Today we're taking our oath. In the meantime we get a lie-in: the alarm clock's set for six o'clock!

10.30 p.m.

It's been extraordinary. We swapped our combats for our ceremonial uniforms, the regiment gathered on the parade ground, there was a great row of officers including the commandant of the base (who we'd never seen). He gave a speech up on a platform and there were letters lit up in fire behind him.

'I swear,' they read.

He told us we were true soldiers now, that the army and the country were depending on us, that we were all as important as each other, whatever role we were now given.

We filed past him one by one, and Inbar Katz handed us a

Bible and a rifle. With our right hands on the Bible and the rifle to our left, we solemnly swore the oath:

'I swear loyalty to Tsahal and to the state of Israel. I swear to serve my country in keeping with her laws. I swear that I shall respect life and protect it.'

Then, very moved by those letters of fire which were still burning, we sang the national anthem Hatikva – hope.

We handed back our equipment and were treated to a little party during which we laughed and cried a lot. It's hard going our separate ways after experiencing so much together.

I learned, not to my surprise, that I'd been appointed to the secret service. I have to report to the base at 11 o'clock on Sunday morning, and I'm not allowed to tell anyone where it is – by word of mouth or in writing. I'll do a three-month course there. Eynat has been posted to a radar unit. She was disappointed but everyone's told her it's exciting. People envy me a bit because the words 'intelligence service' have a buzz of mysterious excitement round them. We'll see about that once we're there.

I might go to Jerusalem this weekend, and I might make love with Jean-David. But there won't be a relationship between us. Apparently in my new unit we only get leave every three weeks. He's not made to be a sailor's wife (unfortunately, you can't really talk about a sailor girl's husband!).

I feel as if I've spent a hundred years in this base. It's lasted barely four weeks. I've got 23 months left: in uniform, at other bases, with other people.

   Maybe that's what being an adult is: getting used to living a life, leaving the place and the people, and starting another life somewhere else.

PART TWO

JERUSALEM, MY LOVE

A soldier indicated a dusty building with a consummately bored wave of his hand, and told me to wait.

'How long?' I asked him.

'You just wait,' he said, perfectly logically. 'You haven't got anything else to do, anyway.'

I put my kit on the ground and sat down against it. I took my book out of my bag and started to read like I hadn't read for a long time. What I mean is I was no longer me, Valérie, I became a character in the book.

I was drawn away from my reading by the feeling that someone was looking at me. How do we sense that sort of thing? Maybe we're so used to other people's indifference that the least sign of interest reaches our brains directly, unhampered by any obstacles on the way.

I looked up. A tall, thin lieutenant of about forty with curly blonde hair was watching me, apparently amazed. I thought she must be my commanding officer and I leapt to my feet, wondering whether I should stand to attention. Oddly, this startled her, as if she'd been caught doing something wrong, and she gave me an apologetic smile and slipped away. I stayed there thoughtfully. In spite of her uniform and her career soldier's stripes, she'd seemed out of place. Her reaction, the way she'd left and the way she'd apologised to a 'rookie' were very strange. I opened my book again, but a shadow fell between me and the sun.

'Valérie? Number 3810159?'

It was a corporal – a very short, slim woman with long hair and a rather ugly face – who'd asked me these questions in a kindly voice.

'Yes.'

'Welcome to our base. Follow me.'

I dragged my kit into a dismal room. A sergeant was sitting behind a desk smoking with her eyes half closed. She was tall with a beautifully clean-cut bob, almond eyes, a fairly strong build and an air of confidence.

'Hello. I'm Tamar, the commanding officer on your course, and this is Romy, my second-in-command.'

Laurel and Hardy, I translated in my head as I saluted them.

'There are ten of you on this course. The others have been instructed to come tomorrow morning. You were asked to come today because you live far away. In any event, you must be outside this building at eight o'clock tomorrow morning. Report to the armoury to pick up your weapon before anything else. I'll give you the release form for it and a permit to leave the base. See you tomorrow.'

Wham! Bam! Such sensitivity, such sophistication in her delivery! At the same time, I thought that the ugly one couldn't simply be kind and the pretty one surly. Too easy, too predictable. I had three months to dig beneath Laurel and Hardy's outer shells . . . I smiled at the thought.

Sergeant Tamar threw me a glance of surprise but said nothing. I saluted again and went out.

Rapid calculation: the base is close to Tel Aviv, and about 120km from Beersheva. Jerusalem, on the other hand, is only 60km away. If I get up very early tomorrow I could be here on time.

About turn to the Holy City. Not to pray, not to moan, not to demonstrate, not to breathe the same air as David, Jesus or Mahomet, nor to buy hideous tourist trinkets in the souk in the old town. Jerusalem because that's where the one I love is, and a little voice is whispering to me that it's now or never.

Free: I feel freer than I ever have in this heavily laden bus gasping along the roads. We've just passed the place known as Shaar Hagaï; the Arabs called it Bab el-Oued. Both names mean the same thing: the gates of the Stream. This was where one of the bloodiest battles of the war of independence was fought in 1948. Military vehicles have been left where they stood on either side of the steeply climbing road to remind travellers of that episode in history. This time I didn't go to sleep, I was bursting with hope and questions: he won't be there, he'll be there, he won't be alone, he'll say 'come here', he'll make up some excuse not to see me, he'll be triumphant when he sees me pitch up with love written all over my face, and he'll laugh at me, he'll take me in his arms, he won't understand why I'm there suddenly. I'll tell him the truth . . . but which truth?

I run my fingers over the barrel of my gun. An Uzi, the weapon they give to girls and jobniks, but Jean-David needn't know that. I want to impress him, to delight him, to seduce him. I want to supersede this girl who took him from me. She's French through and through, she's never done military service, so that's a few points less for her. In some ways I'm counting on Tsahal to help me win back my first love.

At the moment we're at the top of a hill, but – given the size of the hills round here – we're talking mountains. Not that long ago a Palestinian threw himself at the driver of a bus on this line (number 400), sending the whole thing tumbling into the ravine. Net result: 16 dead and a terrible feeling of fear which gripped the whole country. The Egged Company had to spend tens of thousands of shekels to fit the buses with barriers to protect the drivers. A monument was built to the memory of those who died. We're going too quickly so I can't read their names.

We go down the hill and back up another one. Whichever direction you come from, it seems a long and arduous road to Jerusalem.

In the pedestrianised town centre, 5 p.m., the cafes are heaving with people, but then when aren't they? I rang five minutes ago: I got the answerphone and hung up. Two hours and three mochas later he finally answers.

'Hello?' (Still in his thick pseudo-Israeli voice.)

'Jean-David? It's me.'

'Hello, soldier girl! Have you got news from the front?'

'There isn't really a front, you ignorant minor civilian! And anyway, apparently top secret classified news is making the headlines in all the papers. Turn on the TV and switch off the sound, and you'll get a clearer idea of what they're talking about.'

'Where are you calling from?'

'A cafe on Ben-Yehouda Street.'

He's choking, I'm sure he's choking. He finally stops.

'In . . . . in . . . in Jeru?' he stammers, overwhelmed with panic or excitement, I'm finding it hard establishing which.

'Al-Quds* if you prefer or Yerushalayim**. Either way, not that far from where you live, if I remember right. I've got leave till tomorrow morning. I didn't have time to go home so I came here.'

'D'you want . . .'

'. . . to see you, yes, and perhaps to stay the night,' I say, and I add in a whisper, 'If you've got enough room . . .'

'We'll find something. If the worst comes to the worst, the bath's not that uncomfortable. I'm going to go and buy something to feed you. Come in an hour's time. If you've got a lot of stuff take the number 9 bus and get off at the second stop on Aza Street. There's a little road off to the left, that's Berlin Street. On the ground floor of number 14, your servant.'

'Thanks. See you later.'

* Arab name for Jerusalem.
** Hebrew name for Jerusalem.

I close my eyes. Drunk, tense, terrified, impatient, anxious, worried. Praise be to the fact that there's a wide vocabulary to express what I'm feeling at the moment.

16th October, 6.10 a.m.

On the first bus to Tel Aviv.

He opened the door and his eyes lit up, the surprise of the uniform. He opened his arms wide like he was so happy to surrender. I kissed him, I wanted to stay in his arms for hours. He offered me a coffee. I told him about my course, and I laid it on a bit – well, if he doesn't love me at least he can admire me! We ate at his apartment. It's a bit of a couple thing to do: eating in à deux. I didn't dare say that.

Every now and then he would give me these strange looks. I'd give twenty years of my life to know what he thinks of me, but mainly what he feels.

We talked, we didn't talk. He put on Fauré's Requiem *which he loves. I told him it made me feel sad whereas Mozart's* Requiem *gives me a feeling of peace and makes me want to sing. Towards midnight I asked the question, 'Where am I sleeping?'*

He pretended to think and then asked me, 'Where do you want to sleep?'

If I could I would have strangled him and I'd have spent the rest of my life with his murder on my conscience. And all for a bit of bedding, if I can call it that.

I took my courage in both hands.

'There is such a thing as a soldier's right to sleep. I'll sleep

in your bed. If you like, I'd be prepared to make a bit of room for you.'

And off we go! Into bed, children. Good as gold, with T-shirts on. And very tense too, desperate not to touch each other.

He leant over me to say goodnight. He kissed my forehead, my nose, my eyes; I kissed his forehead, his nose, his eyes. We hugged each other very tightly all through the night, stroking each other's faces, sleepily, chastely, like two children who secretly love each other, and it was stronger than making love, it was more beautiful than all the other beautiful moments of my life put together.

I looked at him for a long time before leaving this morning. He opened his eyes and said, 'Look after yourself. Come back and see me.'

I closed the door really quietly, thinking I could die tomorrow and it wouldn't matter. I've had what I wanted from life.

A FIRST DEFEAT

One month of this course already: it's like school to the power of ten. We study from eight in the morning till midnight, with breaks to unwind while we carry out latrine duties here, and kitchen duties there, with the odd two-hour guard duty thrown in to fill any gaps . . .

I've decided not to eat with the others in the refectory any more. I have cheese on toast and a bar of chocolate for lunch every day as I watch the sky which still stays obstinately blue in this khaki world. Long live Resistance! Net result: I've put on two kilos and my friends eye me suspiciously, but I've finished my book and I write, I write about death, about emptiness, about happiness which lasts for just a few moments, about Jean-David, to Jean-David (letters I don't send him). I know he doesn't expect anything from me, and that he definitely doesn't want to know that I love him as much as I dream about him – which is all the time. I've seen that lieutenant from the first day watching me in the distance several times. I've nicknamed her Triple S, 'the spy who spies on the spies'.

There are ten of us, then. Nine from the northern suburbs of Tel Aviv: Daddy's an ambassador, Mummy's a lawyer, Daddy's the chief executive of the Institute of Strategy at Ramat-Gan, Mummy's a journalist, Daddy's a lieutenant colonel, Mummy's at the Ministry of Defence, we have a five-, eight-, ten-bedroom house and we get to the base in the dinky car we were given for our eighteenth.

The tenth girl is from Beersheva. It's a long way away, more than 120km, no one's ever set foot in the place, and anyway no one can think of a good reason to go to such a dump. The girl from Beersheva gets to the base by bus, and sometimes by hitchhiking. Her father's a technician at the aerospace factory, her mother's a pharmacist's assistant at the local chemist. The girl from Beersheva hasn't passed her driving test, keeps her earphones on at night and doesn't deign to eat in the canteen. When her group's on duty, when they have to tidy the room for an inspection she picks up her book and tells the others they should do the same. 'We're given an hour, we rush around like blue-arsed flies, and it's never good enough, we have to start all over again. Why waste our energy doing things to perfection if the officers are never satisfied anyway?' The girls glance at her suspiciously, thinking she doesn't exactly behave like a real soldier, but she's French and, for now, that's sparing her from full-on loathing.

At first I thought I was a mistake, that I'd been put there

inadvertently, or just to make a round number. Apparently not. Apparently I did really well in the psychometric tests I took before I joined the army. To crown it all, I'm top of the 'cherry tomato' intake. A soldier (a male one this time) from another course told me that was what we were called because most of us were less than 1m50 tall, and weighed around 60kg. I'm horribly offended to be associated with the name: I'm 1m62 and I weigh 55kg. Granted, I'm not a bean pole, but I could have been spared comparisons with a spherical tomato, which leaves no room for hope for my looks.

On the first day of the course Sergeant Tamar told us solemnly, 'You've been chosen from thousands of candidates to become part of the military intelligence service. The work you will do every day and the missions you will be trained to carry out are performed by career officers in every army around the world. The country's security lies primarily with you. The least lapse of attention on your part can put the population in danger. Did you know that the Yom Kippur War broke out amid almost total radio silence? The Egyptian planes took off by communicating with a series of simple "clicks". You know what that cost the country.'

We all think about Israel's bloodiest war in respectful silence.

'You will be appointed,' Tamar went on, 'to two services: listening and analysis. You'll have to work as you never have before in your lives so that in just three months you can assimilate as much information as you would in a whole year at school. You have no right to be bad or even mediocre. You must be excellent. Making mistakes and giving up are concepts you will erase from your minds. It's very difficult to get into the intelligence service, but the exit door is open twenty-four hours a day. You are forbidden to talk to anyone about what you learn here. Not to your parents, your friends or even to other soldiers on different courses in this base. Each service is absolutely self-contained, and should remain so. At the end of the course you'll take an oath to the AMAN*. Secrecy is your natural state from now on.'

We're put to work straightaway: maps to learn by heart, overnight, with hundreds of places on them. We have to know every town, village, hamlet, hill, mountain and place name in our neighbouring countries. And also the bases, the radar stations, code names for regiments, for the frequencies used, for the squadrons and the pilots. In a month I've learned a hundred times more about the geography of Jordan, Syria and Iraq than I know about Israel's. We'll mostly be assigned to listening to aircraft. The Jordanian pilots speak in English, a little gift left by the Brits a few decades ago.

There's a daily check of what we've learned the day before. Every Thursday there's a test of the whole week's pro-gramme. There's permanent tension. I would never have believed I could remember so much stuff. Every day I feel as if that's it, I've reached my limits, not one more shred of information can be crammed into my over-laden brain. Not even the chorus of some crass summer hit along the lines of: 'The sun is shining bright/but I'll be with you tonight/Baby,

* Acronym for the military intelligence service.

in your arms/lovin' all your charms.' I feel like when I get out of this place I'll be an amnesiac on anything other than Israel's neighbouring states.

But no. Still the brain goes on recording, and on, and on again. It comes up with memory extensions, a new hard drive every now and then, and at night I find I'm dreaming about Petra, H_4, H_5, Gizeh, Amman, Baghdad, towns and bases I've never seen and I'll never go to because the border's there to separate enemies, but I could place them on a map with my eyes closed.

95. 100. 98, 99, my marks come in, perfect or nearly. Tamar and Romy smile every time they hand my work back. I feel it won't be long before I'll be given a prize as the brightest hope for the intelligence service.

We get leave every fortnight, so I've been out once and I didn't see Rahel who's been posted as a regimental secretary on the Golan Heights near the Syrian border. We write to each other nearly every day. I write to Freddy too, he's massively depressed in prison. Yulia's in military offices in Beersheva, and goes home every evening: she says it feels like she's still at school except she's now getting paid every month. She was looking great, and claims to be knocking the soldiers dead. I had no trouble believing her, she really is gorgeous. I was happy to see her but I found it hard to keep my eyes open.

It's Thursday. I can't wait to get out tomorrow. Rahel will be there, and my sister who I haven't seen for two months.

We're planning to party all weekend. Yulia's got some tickets to see *The Taming of the Shrew*. We also thought we might go to the beach and make the most of the last rays of sunshine before the winter, which usually sets in gently with its 20°C towards December. I think I could also go and see Jean-David. Given how much information I can take on board in twenty-four hours, I should be able to live the equivalent of a whole month in two days.

It's 6 p.m. Tamar and Romy come into our classroom to give us back this morning's test paper. It was about the strength of the Jordanian army and an analysis of an aerial combat during the Six Days' War, and it seemed more difficult than previous ones. Noa, Heidi, Eynat the redhead, Eynat the blonde, Rahel, Hila, Emek, Tsila, Merav and I all turn anxious eyes towards our instructors. They look rather like commanding officers who've just realised their soldiers have organised a karaoke instead of setting up a special mission.

Trying to ward off bad luck, I recite in my head all the marks I've had since the beginning of the course. At worst, I'll get 85 – the lowest mark they'll tolerate. Below that, it starts raining punishments: extra duties, more checks, two or four hours' detention on leave days.

The girls breathe sighs of relief as they get their papers back one after the other. Tamar stops in front of me with a stern expression.

'It's very bad: you've disappointed us,' she blurts out icily.

'We're horribly disappointed,' Romy adds.

(OK, I was wrong: I shouldn't have nicknamed them Laurel and Hardy but Dupont and Dupond from the Tintin books.)

'80,' Tamar says in a sepulchral voice.

'80!' Romy exclaims, as if Tamar has spoken to me in Serbo-Croat and I need a simultaneous translation.

'This is serious. Very, very serious,' says Tamar. 'You can get away with this sort of failure once, but not twice.'

'We've thought about a punishment,' Romy goes on with hypocritical regret. 'You won't have any leave this weekend and you'll do three guard duties. The rest of the time you can come here to revise. You'll be tested on Sunday evening.'

It's the harshest punishment inflicted since the beginning of the course. Nine pairs of eyes are locked on to me. Heidi, Eynat the redhead, Rahel and Hila look devastated, but I wonder whether they're sympathetic or just quaking at the thought of what could happen to them one day. Noa, Eynat the blonde, Emek, Tsila and Merav are wearing quietly satisfied expressions. I stare at the corner of a table, repeating to myself, 'I mustn't cry, I mustn't cry.' The blood's rushed to my head, the tears are pricking in my eyes, ready to spring. If my chin wobbles, that's it, I won't be able to hold back the sobs. So I clamp my chin between my thumb and forefinger, and search desperately for a sentence from a book, a verse from a poem or a piece of music to escape from this moment in which I've not only been accused and judged, but also found guilty. All I can find are the names of bases, code names, names in Arabic or in English, all jumbling together and reeling past my eyes so quickly it's disorientating. I carry on stubbornly, searching compulsively, as if it's a question of life and death, I piece together Jean-David's face in my mind's eye, in a blinding blaze of light, and I hear a chorus singing for me:

Requiem æternam dona eis, Dominæ: et lux perpetua luceat eis. Te decet hymnus, Deus, in Sion, et tibi reddetur votum in Jerusalem. Exaudi orationem meam, ad te omnis caro veniet. Requiem æternam dona eis, Dominæ, et lux perpetua luceat eis*.

Mozart's *Requiem*. I can hear it as if hundreds of musicians and choristers have landed in our base and are playing it for me. I'm saved. I even manage to relax my jaw and look my instructors right in the eye.

'It's nothing,' I murmur. 'Of course I'll study the whole weekend, and I'll make up for this on Sunday.'

Tamar looks perplexed. Romy's adopted a delighted expression. My heart's going to give in in thirty seconds but I have to hold out till this evening, late this evening. Right up until I'm in bed and can listen to the *Requiem* for real. Crying at last.

I rang home. I put on a very bright voice to say, 'You won't believe your luck! A month without seeing me or having

---

* Lord, give unto them eternal rest and let the light everlasting shine on them. God, it is in Zion that thy praises are sung worthily; in Jerusalem that Thou art given sacrifices. Hear my prayer, Thou to whom all mortals go. Lord, give unto them eternal rest and let the light everlasting shine on them.

to wash my uniform, that's like a summer holiday for parents!' Mum was beside herself. She suggested ringing the base commandant to tell him it was scandalous locking away her daughter who'd had the best grades on the course so far, that we weren't ruled by Hitler or Stalin and that, objectively, I hadn't committed a crime, I'd even got a good mark.

'It happens to everyone,' I said, trying to calm her down. 'It's not a drama. It's already been a fortnight since my last leave, there's just another fortnight to go, it'll go quickly . . . Pretend I've gone off across the United States in a jeep, I'll try and think that too.'

I rang Yulia, who did her best to console me. I told her to let Rahel know that I'd try and get hold of her at six o'clock the next day.

I didn't ring Jean-David. I wouldn't have been able to speak to him. Too many sentences blocked in my throat. I'd have had to be able to tell him that I loved him, that I wanted him to write to me and to come and see me. He would probably have been very kind to me, very comforting. But not loving. I've got more strength to cope with silence than with pity.

Pity is something the girls I share a room with have got by the truck-load – even the ones who looked pleased earlier on. Heidi offers to leave me her store of biscuits, Noa gives me her favourite tape, Hila gives me a hug and says in her cartoon voice (which made us roar with laughter in the early days), 'It'th really not fair. We've all thcored 80. And we've never been punished like thith.'

'But it's precisely because she's the best,' murmurs Rahel, the calmest, most thoughtful and measured of us all.

'You're going to have the dormitory to yourself, it's almost like a suite at the Hilton!' Eynat the redhead says in a singsong voice.

'And you do know that the cook surpasses himself at the weekends,' Eynat the blonde adds maliciously.

I look at them as if discovering them for the first time. Feeling slightly ashamed, I realise that I dismissed them all straightaway as 'Daddy's girls'. It's true, though, they've been particularly spoiled by life, they have all the things I still don't see myself having in twenty years' time. That doesn't stop them having a bit of imagination, and being able to understand what I'm going through, at least today.

I decide to make an effort and eat with them in the canteen the next day. I'll have plenty of time to be alone this weekend.

Even so, I couldn't help feeling a little bit heavy-hearted when I saw them leaving with their big bags full of dirty washing. Pariah, black sheep, parasite: humiliating words trotted through my head. And the inadmissible (which I can confide only to Rahel): the fear of being expelled from the course if I commit the same offence again. That terror has invaded my whole body: it's something everyone's frightened of, on every course in the army. In fact, in Hebrew you say you 'fall' from a course, in the same way that to fall means to die. I'm going to hang on, grit my teeth and study really intensively, like I said yesterday. I'm going to bury the pain of not seeing the people I need most in the world. I don't know if I like it here, but I know I'm proud to have been selected to be in the intelligence service. So I have to stay, no matter what.

A FEAR THAT DOESN'T SPEAK ITS NAME

I've spent the weekend between the classroom, the guard-room and the phone box. When the girls got back they found me very tired. But I've passed the test, I'm pretty sure, and Tamar's face confirms it this Monday morning: she hands me the paper with a nod of her head.

'92. That's not bad, but it would be better if you went back to your original grades.'

Romy pouts, unconvinced. 'It's borderline. Especially given you had two days to work on it.'

There's a sort of note of triumph in her voice. What exactly does she expect? For me to fail again, for me to 'fall'? I'd really like to ask her but I'd be running too many risks: you can't mess with the hierarchy and that's a shame, it means there's no room for frankness in relationships. I have to swallow my questions and stare dead ahead. There's just one figure, 100, that I want to achieve come what may, every time, from today. I plunge frenetically into a comparative study of the F-5 and the F-1 combat aircraft.

It was chicken thighs for supper – and that's the greatest luxury in army canteens – but I wasn't hungry. Right now we're heading back up to our classroom and I feel brutally hot, really hot. I rush to my seat, I try to take a good deep breath but nothing makes any difference. The blood's flowing up to my head and not flowing back down. I'm beginning to suffocate. I take off my glasses and try to fight against this invisible, unknown thing, but it's even worse. I want to call for help, my face is paralysed, I can't move my lips, I've got pins and needles in my cheeks. I hear someone cry, 'Look, Valérie's not feeling well!'

'Valérie! Valérie? Can you talk?'

No, I can't talk, and I tell them with my eyes that I'm panicking, that I'm very frightened I'm going to die in the next few minutes, that they must save me.

Someone runs past me shouting, 'Quick! Call Tamar and Romy!'

I stop moving, for fear of tightening the vice which is crushing my head and heart. Tamar and Romy loom up in front of me. They try to help me take a few steps, but I'm hopelessly paralysed. What I see worries me even more: the panicky expression on Romy's face and the serious one on Tamar's.

I'm laid down on a stretcher. The infirmary. A nurse with a drawling voice takes my blood pressure and asks, 'Wheeeeere does it huuuuuurt?'

I point to my head, and try to articulate a few words.

'I feel wrung out. Like I've crossed the ocean in a raging storm.'

She remains impassive: she wants precise details, something concrete.

'But what exactly happened?'

'I was very hot and . . .'

I stop dead. It's starting again: the pain awakens somewhere in my body and rises up to my head, amplifying every second and filling my skull which is about to explode. I'm a bomb. I sob without any tears. I clutch my head in my hands and wail, 'It's coming back, it's coming back! Oh no! Do something! Help me! No! No! It hurts! It hurts too much!'

I'm terrified, and the nurse is even more so than me.

'Avi, Avi!' she calls, 'come quickly!'

A soldier appears, glances at us quickly to establish which of us is in the worse state, sensibly decides that I am, and squeezes my hand to reassure me while, with his other hand, he dials a phone number.

'An ambulance. Straightaway. We need to take a soldier to casualty.'

That soldier is me. And I'm suffering like I've never suffered before, and I'm discovering to my amazement that you can be in a huge amount of pain and still be lucid. Still see everything, hear everything and, therefore, be frightened.

The ambulance sets off at full tilt, with the siren piercing my eardrums. I'm writhing in pain, and crying and moaning. *What's happening to me? Am I going to die without seeing the people I love?*

Yichilov Hospital. The pain has retreated to its lair again, taking all my strength with it. I look for it, watching out for it. The fact that it's not there worries me. Where will it spring from next time? And what unbearable level will it soar to?

They take my blood pressure again. They do an electro-cardiogram and take some blood. They talk to me gently, as if to a child, but I'm too exhausted to understand. They give me a pill and settle me in a room next to an old man with a very dark complexion and pale eyes. I don't know why but I feel terribly pained by the sight of him. That's the last thought to cross my mind before I sink into a dense sleep.

When I wake up a nurse tells me that I'm better, that I'll be able to go back to the base today. The man in the neighbouring bed is no longer there. I ask for news of him but she doesn't answer. I try to find out what happened to me, but she still won't speak. Or hardly.

'It will all be explained to you in good time.'

There's another one who must have sworn secrecy a few years ago.

They give me my discharge papers and two pills that I should take in the event of another attack. I turn the pack over: Valium. I've always thought that was a drug, I wouldn't have thought a hospital would just hand it out.

The soldier-nurse from the base is waiting for me. She looks at me as if she's terrified of me. She winds me up:

what's the point of trying to make other people better if you're such a sissy yourself?

'I've got rabies,' I announce (to give her a good reason to quake like that). 'I've been given a tranquilliser but the effects will wear off in a quarter of an hour.'

Her eyes open wide in an expression of total horror. She insists on sitting down at the front next to the ambulance driver, leaving me on my own in the back. That's exactly what I wanted: I want to be alone and to think, but however hard I try, the mechanism in my brain seems to be incontrovertibly blocked.

Ronit – that's the name the guard gave the nurse when we drove into the base – quickly settles me in my room and flees, mumbling, 'Your instructor will come and see you. Get some rest.'

I wait impatiently for Tamar. She might be able to throw some light on things for me. It's Romy who comes tiptoeing into the room, looking very awkward. She explains, with all sorts of convolutions, that she doesn't know exactly what happened to me.

'It's probably a sort of turn because you were very stressed and very tired. You can rest here at the base today, of course. We'll see whether you can get back to your lessons tomorrow . . .'

'I imagine the powers that be aren't going to extend their kindness to giving me leave so that I can go home for a few days . . .'

I said this with a little smile. I can tell that my 'condition' means I can say what I like with complete impunity. I could tell Romy right now that I think she's ugly, hypocritical and stupid and that it's outrageous that she should have the same name as someone I once knew and really liked . . . and she'd look at me sympathetically and tell me I should rest.

Freedom is a kind of madness which means you can tell people exactly what you think of them without running many risks.

'The girls will come and see you soon. They've been very worried about you,' she says with a reproachful note in her voice: she can't help holding this against me. As far as she's concerned, I'm just trying to get attention. To spare myself more of the same, I close my eyes. In every book I've read and every film I've seen, that's what people do when they're very ill and they want to show that they'd like to be left alone because they can no longer bear the pitiful expressions of the healthy people around them. Romy has apparently been to the cinema in her life (which I reckon must be a pretty mediocre one), because she slips away immediately, fairly relieved to end our conversation there.

The girls come into the room one by one. They look serious.

'We were bloody terrified,' Heidi exclaims.

'Oh yes,' Noa agrees, 'you were completely, completely . . .'

'. . . purple,' Rahel finishes for her, staring at me oddly.

'What did they tell you at the hospital?' Emek asks pragmatically.

'Nothing.'

I'm beginning to feel guilty. How can an earthquake not be

anything? If you can't pin some medical term on what I've been through it's as if nothing actually happened.

Noa looks urgently at the others.

'It's supper time,' she says. 'Shall we bring you something?'

'No, thanks. I'm not hungry.'

The only thing I can do, and that I want to do, is to sleep, to sleep and to stop existing. To stop seeing that fear that I suddenly seem to inspire in them all.

I didn't hear Tamar come into the room. She left a note on my blanket:

Get some rest, tomorrow's another day.

I've decided to get back to my lessons very quickly. If I miss another day, I'm going to break all records for inadequacy on the course by getting a mark below fifty, and that would make me ill for the rest of my days.

We've started our lessons on listening to the airwaves, with bulky earphones over our heads. It's a tape recording which we have to decipher as it goes along, writing on a travel warrant with the words 'highly confidential' at the top of the page. It's of Jordanian pilots in training, and the dialogue is fascinating.

Hunter One, clear for take-off.

Roger.

Hunter Two, clear for take-off.

Roger.

There are four of them. They've all taken off.

Hunter One to Hunter Two, channel one eight, go!

They're changing frequency.

Hunter One to Hunter Two, Three, Four, do you hear me?
Loud and clear.
OK. Let's go to five thousand feet.
Five thousand feet, Roger.

They arrange themselves in combat formation. The squadron leader manages the operations with all the efficiency of a stage director, placing each plane as if it were on a chessboard. *Hunter Three* is playing the role of the target. *Hunter Two* has to lead it up to 7,000 feet, while *Hunter Four* executes a loop the loop in order to position itself right in the line of fire.

Hunter One to Hunter Four, do you see the target?
Fox one.
OK, fire!

The exercise is over. Aerial combat lasts two minutes on average. *Hunter Four* is singing in Arabic, clearly very pleased with himself.

We're all smiling broadly: what we've learned about the techniques used in combat means that we can 'see' the planes. It's like magic. And it's also intoxicating to be what everyone has always dreamed of being at some time: a fly on the wall who can see and hear everything without anyone knowing. Soon, in a few weeks, we'll spend every day with *Hunter One* and his friends. Right now I find it very hard imagining that they're our 'enemies'.

At the end of the day Tamar gave me a note summoning me to the headquarters the next day. I have to meet an officer, one Ronen Tal, at 5.30 p.m. The headquarters are based in Tel Aviv. I have four hours' leave. Whatever comes out of this meeting I'm so worried about, at least I will have had a nice break.

FREUD COMES TO MY RESCUE

I've been through three different checkpoints where they examined my papers minutely. I've been put into a large room which is more like the waiting room for a Parisian doctor than a military office. I open a book, but what I'm really thinking about is who this Tal Ronen is, or is it Ronen Tal? They're both first names. I prepare myself for the worst and for the best.

The worst: he informs me coldly that I've been taken off the course. Too much is too much. A low mark followed by some fit that no one understands would be enough to see me relegated to secretarial work or the kitchens.

The best: Ronen Tal is in charge of the military intelligence service and he wants to entrust me with an important mission.

My grasp of reality nudges me towards the worst. The dreams I treat myself to twenty-four hours a day whisper to me that every hope is legitimate.

A door opens and a man comes into the room. He's average height, slim, very tanned, with an appealingly receding hairline, about forty, pretty attractive (I won't describe him any further, I think I've made it clear enough that I find the Ronen Tal in question rather good-looking). There is one striking detail, here on the sixth floor of the headquarters building: he's not in uniform.

He holds out his hand to me and shows me into a magnificent office. There are two swivel leather armchairs facing each other across a wide desk. The lights of Tel Aviv glitter through a huge bay window.

'Hello, I'm Lieutenant Colonel Ronen Tal. I run the psychology unit for Tsahal. Do you know why you've been asked here?'

'I've got a fairly clear idea.'

'Tell me about this attack – what you felt and thought.'

I launch into a long description, starting with the punishment which had been so appalling for me: being deprived of my fortnightly freedom. I had felt that I was suffocating when Tamar pronounced the words which added up to: 'You won't be taking the number 370 bus home, you won't be sleeping in your own room which isn't a dormitory but a proper room with posters on the walls and postcards of places you've never been to but you dream of visiting one day, you won't eat meals cooked in human-sized saucepans (as opposed to Gulliver-proportioned cauldrons), you won't go clubbing with your friends, you won't go to the beach, you won't chat to Rahel for hours to catch up on each other's lives (knowing you never will but hoping to anyway), you won't go and see Jean-David.'

After saying Jean-David's name I look down. I've said too much: what has this got to do with him? But he's clearly interested in everything because he goes on to ask, 'How do you feel about being in the army?'

I sigh.

'F . . . fine.'

'You seem to hesitate.'

'No, it's just the answer's rather complicated.'

'I've got however long it takes.'

'I haven't.'

He raises an eyebrow questioningly.

'I have to be back at the base in two hours,' I explain, to remind him that we're in the army and not quietly getting to know each other in some pub in Ireland.

He brushes my explanation aside with his right hand, as if to say, 'Stuff that, I'll deal with that.'

He seems insistent so I carry on.

'Right. I'm going to speak frankly: I feel fine and not fine. I know that's a bit of an easy answer but it's the absolute truth. I'm proud to wear the uniform because it represents the history I've been taught, because it's the uniform of heroes, because I've spent my teenage years with my friends trying to imagine what sort of soldiers we'd make. I know that, by being in the army like everyone else, I'll really become part of this country. I'm also glad I'm in the intelligence service, I feel I'm actually going to be of some use, and I really enjoy the lessons. At the same time, the system's so rigid it gets me down. I know discipline is essential but I would have thought that if we were given a little more time and freedom, if we weren't forced to make our beds again three times, just as a matter of principle, we'd still be just as good as soldiers. And a bit happier with life.'

Then I add, 'Well, I don't know about the others . . . but, as far as I'm concerned, I would be.'

Lieutenant Colonel bigwig in the army psychology unit seems to be deep in thought about what I've just said.

'What does being a woman mean to you?' he asks suddenly.

I can't see what that's got to do with anything but I don't dare say that. If he's trying to get my clothes off, he's gone about it the wrong way: the question just makes me laugh.

'Being a woman? It means living more intensely than a man, because we have very powerful physical experiences. It's wanting to change the world, which has put us to one side for a good few thousand years. And it's also being a complement to men.'

He seems to like my answer. He carries on with his little interrogation, hopping from one subject to another, from my parents to my taste in music, from what makes me laugh (the way the children and the old are so naive, subtle humour) to what makes me cry (other people's despair, hopeless situations, a lack of love, books and films with sad endings). From what frightens me (fire, being powerless in the face of pain, violence, not being loved by a man I love) to what disgusts me (injustice, any form of injustice). From my good qualities (tenacity, loyalty, impatience) to my faults (too much pride, a kind of egotism, impatience – again). From what I would be prepared to die for (I don't think I am ready to die at eighteen) to what makes me want to live (my dreams, my longing to realise them, the books I haven't read, the ones I want to write, the emotions I've experienced and have yet to experience, sunsets, life as I want to live it).

I'd willingly stay in this office for hours: no one's been this interested in me for at least fifteen years, but all good things come to an end.

'Well, Valérie, you're going to go back to your base and you'll see your course through to the end. There's an officer at the base who's a psychologist, she's extremely good. You can go and see her if you'd like to, from time to time, for a chat. It might help you cope with everything that's a bit too much for you. Her name's Shlomit Dror.' (Is this a sign? Shlomit is the feminine of 'shalom' which means 'peace', and Dror means 'freedom'.)

I get up and hold out my hand: even though he's very high-ranking I think it would be ridiculous to give a military salute to someone who now knows all the basics about me. His handshake is firm and friendly.

'Good luck,' he says, and then hesitates for a moment before adding, 'You'll see, I'm sure things will get better rather than worse.'

I smile. I feel so light: I've offloaded half a ton of angst in his office and he doesn't even seem to mind.

Back at the base, I ask Tamar whether I can see Lieutenant Shlomit Dror. She doesn't bat an eyelid but tells me that she'll let me know as soon as possible. I concentrate on a session listening to Bluesky Squadron who are training in combat against Blackbird Squadron.

That afternoon Tamar hands me a Form 524b: *Number 3810159 has a meeting with Lieutenant Shlomit Dror at 10.30 tomorrow morning.*

We're meant to be on kitchen duty – I'll get out of some of it. That's something gained already!

Shlomit Dror's office is in a small prefabricated building which stands out from every other building on the base because it has window boxes with geraniums in them hanging from the windows. I'm two minutes early. At precisely ten-thirty a tall, slim woman of about forty with curly blonde hair opens the door. Which of us is the more surprised? Perhaps she is – she's watched me so often reading, right from the day I arrived. She holds out her hand to me. In the more than two months that I've been in the army, she's the second person to do this to me. I find it profoundly comforting in this world when bringing your hand up to your temple is *de rigueur*.

'Hello, I'm Shlomit Dror.'

'Valérie Zenatti. The note said we should meet.'

She shows me strange drawings with lots of thick black lines creating shapes which I have to interpret. Then I tell her what brought me here, the attack that no one's been prepared to give a name to. She opens a file and tells me that it was a syndrome commonly known as HYG, from the English words Hot Young Girl.

I think about the words and say indignantly, 'That's a pretty humiliating name!'

She agrees with me, but she's keen to explain.

'It's a combination of spasmodic paralysis known as tetany and, in your case, a violent migraine. And it is true that it's a syndrome that affects girls more than boys.'

I'm moderately satisfied by her explanation.

'You know,' she adds gently, 'sometimes our bodies express things we can't seem to say.'

Hearing this, without any warning, I start to shake and burst into tears.

The course is coming to an end. Two weeks after my attack we were treated to a cultural outing: an experimental play which I didn't understand at all, performed by soldier-actors. The army really is a khaki version of society: there are soldier-cooks, soldier-drivers, soldier-singers, soldier-journalists, soldier-switchboard-operators, soldier-psychologists and even soldier-primary-schoolteachers sent into schools in 'developing towns'.

We recently discovered that there were three possible postings for us at the end of the course: two bases, one in the North and one in the South, known as 'closed' bases (which means the soldiers stay at the bases for fifteen days in succession and then have five days' leave), and one base near Jerusalem called an 'open' base where you can go out as long as you're not on guard duty or any other kind of duty. I've been led to understand, given where my parents live, that

I'm likely to be posted to the South. I quake at the thought, for a thousand and one reasons which go by two names: my own freedom and Jean-David.

For the first time in my life I've decided to be coldly calculating and to use Shlomit Dror, who I see twice a week to escape from the infernal routine and because it's so good talking to someone who really listens. I'm also convinced that everything that's said in her office is carefully noted and transmitted to the powers that be should the need arise. They wouldn't run the risk keeping on depressives, neurotics and anyone displaying other forms of hysteria. So I pepper our conversations with sentences like: 'If I were in a closed base, I'd suffocate again.' 'If I were in an open base I wouldn't suffer so much.'

I'm a bit ashamed of myself for betraying the woman who gives me regular encouragement, who thinks it's a good thing not to be like everyone else, that there's nothing wrong with wanting to look at the sky and the clouds or wanting to read instead of swallowing down insipid meals. But I feel as if my survival depends on this wretched posting and I'm sure that, deep down, the one person who has it in her power to save me isn't completely duped.

When I was last home on leave, there was a letter for me that had been posted in Paris: Jean-David writing to tell me he was in France for Christmas and the New Year and that he was going skiing. He said rather enigmatically, 'I often think about a little soldier girl who thinks she's weak, but I know she's strong.' He ended the letter with: 'Another smile, J-D.'

After re-reading it several times I knew the letter by heart, but I still read it a hundred times more while I listened to one of Jean-David's favourite songs.

As I did every year at that time, I felt incredibly nostalgic for the Christmas shop windows. How can we live such different lives on the same planet? Partying in one place but not another? I saw the new year in doing guard duty and drinking a nasty cup of black coffee in a paper cup. Emek, the only smoker in our group, who was on guard duty with me, made a firework by throwing her cigarette against a tree trunk and we wished each other a happy new year.

I'm concentrating all my intellectual energies on the lessons, which are becoming more and more intensive, and the rest of the time I spend alone. The girls are eyeing me guardedly again. Ever since my attack they really don't understand me at all. The army and its laws are so obvious to all of them, they suckled on the logic of duty on their parents' laps (their parents were all, without exception, either career soldiers or reservists). My father spent the Algerian war of independence doing guard duties outside cinemas, which made a considerable contribution to his cinematographic education. He's unbeatable on any film which came out between 1960 and 1962, but when he talks to me about the French army (a masculine world of smutty jokes) I have trouble finding any connection with what I'm experiencing. My mother, on the other hand, has never worn a uniform or touched a weapon, which is completely normal anywhere else in the world.

We swore an oath to the secret service today. The ceremony took place at the base, near the little museum dedicated to Yonatan Netanyahou, the hero of the elite unit who died in the operation at Entebbe*. I was impressed by the juxta-position. Mum was there, looking very proud, with Yulia, Rafi, Ilan and Freddy (who I hadn't seen since he was released). He's lost weight but prison didn't succeed in putting out the light in his eyes or in changing his voice. He sang me an Arik Einstein song full of hope and joie de vivre. I felt fit to burst I was so happy. It was so good seeing them again and – through them – finding the me that I know (cheerful and loved) in this place where I felt I was going to have to spend a whole eternity alone. And so to the course: I allowed myself the little luxury of coming first, I was given the unit's green and white insignia and, crucially, crucially, I've been posted to the base near Jerusalem! Thank you, Shlomit.

* In 1976 an Air France flight from Paris to Tel Aviv was diverted by German terrorists sympathetic to the Palestinian revolutionary movement. The plane was sent to Entebbe in Uganda. The Jewish and Israeli passengers were held hostage and the others were released. The French crew insisted on staying with the hostages. The Israeli secret services carried out an impressive rescue opera-tion, applauded by the Western world. The episode has become known as 'Operation Entebbe'.

CORPORAL, AND PROUD OF IT

Hammer One to Hurricane One, clear for take-off.
Hammer One to Hurricane Two, clear for take-off.
Hammer One to Hurricane Three, clear for take-off.
Hurricane One to Hurricane Two, Three, channel 29, go!
Roger, channel 29.
'Frequency 29, frequency 29!' I cry, and I put down my pen.

It's a week now since we arrived in this tiny base bristling with strange antennae, perched on a rocky hill and with a Palestinian village down below us. We 'work' in a bunker sorely lacking in aesthetic appeal. Paradox: we listen to everything that's going on in the sky but we can't see it at all. The first time we went into the 'Printing Press' (the code name given to our listening post), our eyes opened wide as we stared: there were twenty or so soldiers sitting at tape recorders with earphones over their heads. Facing them, on a raised platform, there were four people (three of whom were from the air force) taking notes and giving instructions. On another platform, a little further away, two soldiers – also with earphones on – tapped away on computer keyboards. They smiled at our astonished faces and went back to their activities as if nothing had happened.

At the moment we're working in duplicate, connected up to the same tape recorders as the previous intake who check that we don't get confused between conversations between pilots and the latest Madonna single. We're meant to be operational in a week, and there are about ten people in the old intake just finishing their tour of duty (and these are all girls because the boys have another whole year to do . . . and it feels as if, for once, they wouldn't mind a bit of sexual equality). That's how the groups replace each other, in a never-ending sequence, with the newcomers gradually becoming the old hands as their predecessors move on.

We do three eight-hour shifts. Morning, afternoon and night, this place has been permanently occupied for decades. No plane takes off from Jordanian soil without our knowing about it, and I find the idea fascinating.

Each tape machine is tuned into a frequency: control towers, radar stations or pilot training frequencies. As soon as a plane changes frequency, we let everyone know and someone takes over on another set. We inform the air force of any activities which strike us as unusual, and they in turn inform a central office which collates all the information gathered by the various units. In the evening we decode everything on the day's significant tapes and we analyse the pilots' combat techniques and what they've learned.

Up on the small platform, one soldier's screen flashes up the frequencies as soon as they're activated. He's the 'second pair of ears', the one that comes in as a reinforcement when the dialogue's almost inaudible. It's usually a soldier who's already been here for at least six months. Beside him, another soldier goes through all the frequencies with a fine-tooth comb to try and detect the ones that have just come into use.

In a few days we've already got to know all the unit's funny ways. The favourite posts are on the international airport in Amman where you can also listen in on pilots on regular flights from all over the world. I smiled for a whole day after hearing an Air France pilot with a strong French accent (he was speaking in English) coming into Jordanian airspace.

'*Air Frrrance 369 flyeeeng from Pareees to Barrrrhain, seeex souzand feet.*'

'*AF 369, six thousand feet, OK, bon voyage!*'

The second favourite post for the soldiers in the 'Printing Press' is the pilot school. They get bollocked by their instructors the whole time, it's very funny. We sympathise with them, we know they're the same age as us.

Finally, each tape recorder has a name which is inscribed on it in felt tip. People almost come to blows to have the privilege of inventing more and more ridiculous names for them. We've already been treated to 'Radio silence', 'Arranged marriage', 'Ketchup and chocolate', 'Kitchen lieutenant', 'Babbling Beatles', 'Spud battles', 'Lame pilot', 'Sleep it off', 'Noa's gorgeous', 'Hussein's eyes', 'Two years' holiday' . . .

I feel good. Finally useful, in the real world at last. Tomorrow we'll be celebrating four months in the army, and we'll be promoted to corporals by our commanding officer, Ouri.

The ceremony took place in the courtyard outside the refectory. Ouri, who's of American origin, pinned the two stripes of white fabric on to us.

'Private Valérie Zenatti, I name you Corporal in Tsahal, the Israeli army, and I hope you will honour your new rank.'

Eynat the redhead was last to be decorated. We were all still standing to attention when streams of water, a few dozen eggs and several kilos of flour were hurled down on us. We started screaming so loudly that one of the two soldiers on watch ran over, thinking the base was being attacked. Ouri collapsed with laughter and the old intake came out of hiding singing, 'Mazal Tov! Mazal Tov*!'

We swore at them copiously and chased them all over the base to wipe the muck off on their clean uniforms. Gil, one of the old hands, slapped us on the back, singing, 'Now you're one of u-us! Now you're one of u-us!'

Ouri asked us to come back to attention, claiming that the ceremony was not yet over, and someone took a picture of us all. The 'cherry tomatoes' looked a proud bunch, soaked to the skin, our faces powdered with flour, and egg yolk in our hair!

'OK, girls,' Ouri said, 'you can have a shower if you really insist. Anyone who's not in the alert group has leave until

* Congratulations!

ten o'clock this evening.'

Lucky me, I was in the alert group the day before. I'm off to conquer Jerusalem.

The soldier who picked me up hitchhiking drops me near Mont-Scopus university. The city's already shrouded in darkness, night falls at about 4 p.m. in winter. I wait for the bus with dozens of students barely older than myself. As always when I come out of the base, I feel as if I've gone through something like the Iron Curtain and stepped into the free world. 'Civilians' have the choice of not getting up in the morning. When they do the washing-up they wash about three plates, not seventy. No one wakes them at two in the morning to do guard duty. They dress however they want to . . .

The bus trundles slowly into the centre, travelling through the religious quarters where dark shadows hurry through the streets to go to evening prayer.

I ring Jean-David from the same cafe as last time. Superstition settles in me somewhere. A man's voice answers, sleepy and unfamiliar.

'I share the apartment with him,' it tells me. 'He said he wouldn't be back tonight.'

'Is he working?'

'No, I don't think so. Well, I'm not his nursemaid, I don't know.'

I hang up. My thoughts are playing ping pong in my head. He's with someone.

He's out with friends.

He's in love with someone else.

He's staying at a friend's house.

He doesn't even know I exist any more.

He's waiting to hear from me.

I try to reason with myself out loud (I often do this): Right, you're going to ruin your bit of freedom over this. What do you think? That he spends his life glued to the phone, waiting patiently for it to ring and for it to be you? Come on, you're dreaming! He's getting on with his life. You'd do the same thing in his shoes. (I try to protest timidly, but the voice goes on firmly:) Go on, walk about. Look how beautiful the stonework is! Doesn't your heart beat a little faster just hearing the name Jerusalem? This is where you'll come the minute you're out of the base, it's the first post of your freedom and you'll come back to it time and again. You're going to get to know this place, and you're going to learn to love it like everyone who's loved it before you: passionately.

I stop talking (I've decided I'm pretty good company for myself). I often encourage myself like this, with one part of me talking to another. The 'real' Valérie, the fragile, disorientated one, listens meekly to the other Valérie, the one who has an answer to everything, the one who never gives up, the one who shakes people awake with a lyrical – but still convincing – voice.

I go up Ben-Yehouda Street, then turn left into King George Street which goes down towards the Montefiori mill. I know that from there you get the prettiest view of the ramparts of the Old Town. In Jerusalem you never stop going up and down, the place is built on a thousand hills. If you're down below you can't help climbing up, and if you're at the top you have no choice but to go down: as far as your legs are concerned it's a whole lesson in hope and humility in one city.

'A sort of physical philosophy,' I whisper to myself. I haven't even noticed that the route I've taken to admire the ramparts is exactly the route the number 9 bus takes to get to Jean-David's apartment. Only once you get to France Square you have to turn right instead of going straight ahead. On my left there's a road going off down the hill. An inscription catches my eye: Alliance Française. I know this is an organisation set up in the nineteenth century to promote French culture. The white stone building looks welcoming: a flight of steps, a little porch area and large noticeboards on which someone's written by hand, *As part of the celebrations for the anniversary of the French Revolution, the Jerusalem Alliance Française is screening an episode of* Apostrophes* *this evening.* I push the door open: the ramparts of Jerusalem – which date a good deal further back than the French Revolution – will have to wait a bit longer.

I take out a membership of the Alliance (at a reduced rate for military personnel) – now I can come to screenings of French films and use their library. I feel euphoric: so long as I have books within arm's reach, nothing too terrible can happen to me.

---

* A television programme on literature and the arts.

There are about ten of us in the little projection room. I am fascinated by the programme, by how cultured the guests are, how civil and impassioned. I remember as a child hearing one of them arguing in favour of abolishing the death penalty. I tell myself I want to be like him: to have that strength and calm, that conviction for serving a just cause.

In Israel all the extremes of society live side by side, though not always easily. There are some people who are too rich and others who are shamefully poor; shadows who rock as they pray to God, and silhouettes in miniskirts who dance, thinking of their own pleasure and living for the moment; militants who want peace now, and who know that to achieve that we would have to give the Palestinians the right to live as they want to; and others who swear their loyalty to the Land and to the Bible, who block their ears and cover their eyes to the fact that 3,000,000 Palestinians live – not especially well – in Gaza, in the hills of Judea and Samaria. The tensions also grow worse every day between the religious fanatics who insist on closing a particular cinema in Jerusalem on Saturdays and the laymen who criticise them for not doing military service; between the unemployed who demonstrate their despair outside Parliament and the high-tech engineers; between the Moroccan Jews and the Russian Jews; between the left-wing militants and the right-wing militants who hurl abuse and hatred at each other: 'Assassins!' cry the ones, 'Traitors!' reply the others.

And the blood flows, flows in the territories and in Jerusalem – where every now and then a Palestinian labourer throws an axe or a hand knife at Israelis, crying, 'Allah

Akhbar!', God is great. Some even say that we could do with a good war to wash away all this tension. But what exactly is a 'good' war?

In the country where I live, there are a thousand revolutions to be fought.

THE WAR OF STONES

For the first time in many weeks the whole group is back on leave in Beersheva, and we're sitting out on the grass practically under my bedroom window. Rahel's come down from the Golan Heights, where she works as a secretary in an armoured unit, although her work is far from being secretarial. She's a psychiatrist, friend, older sister and confidante to the soldiers. She has to organise parties, outings and birthday celebrations for various people. She comforts and consoles, in other words she provides the female touch in an entirely male unit.

She tells us about the play she put on with her soldiers, entitled *The Cook is Our Worst Enemy*.

'The script was so funny. Everyone wanted a part, including the commandant and the cook, who did his best to fight his corner.' She seems so happy. I'm sure she feels much happier in a boys' unit than in a mixed one.

When Freddy came out of prison he didn't want to go back to his old unit. He was appointed driver for a commandant in the Southern region, based at Beersheva.

'One day I happened to be singing when he was around and ever since then he asks me for at least two songs per trip – he says it helps him concentrate. His daughter's getting married in two months and he's asked me to sing at the reception.'

We all clap and congratulate him, happy that our friend's talents have been recognised by a lieutenant colonel.

Ilan is in the Givati unit in Gaza.

'I don't want to talk about it,' he says. 'I already live with it twenty-four hours a day. Luckily, I'm allowed to play the guitar; thanks to that I've got plenty of friends.'

Ilana is a nurse in an all-male base.

'I've got them all at my feet,' she announces as we listen in open-mouthed amazement. 'Some of them want to be signed off sick, but others want the exact opposite, to have their weaknesses hidden.'

She seems very pleased with her little bit of power. Rahel, Yulia and I exchange a look: you don't mean Paint-pot's become a bit of a star?

'They're all at my feet too,' Yulia sparks, '. . . but not for that sort of reason,' she simpers, coiling a lock of hair round a finger. 'And I'm not the one serving them coffee, they offer it to me,' she adds triumphantly.

She closes her eyes and drags on her cigarette. She's started smoking recently, to the horror of the whole group (we're massively anti-smoking). I'll probably go to hell for this, but

I'm going to say it anyway: cigarettes just add to her air of confidence.

They start turning their attention to me, waiting for me to tell them something about my life as a soldier.

'Umm . . . no one's grovelling at my feet, and the rest is classified top secret. Sometimes it changes and becomes "ultra secret",' I add to make it sound more interesting.

'You're weird,' Yulia interjects. 'Are you really not allowed to tell us?'

No, I can't tell them anything. What I enjoy most at the base is what I do there, it's the moment a pilot announces '*Fox one*' during an exercise, which means he's hit the target a first time. I imagine he's happy then, pleased with himself, and I feel a small share of that pleasure. The voices have become familiar to me, and I try and imagine the faces hiding behind them. Eynat the redhead's even fallen in love with one of the instructors, whose code name is *Eagle One*. She can't wait for the awards ceremony for the current course which will be aired on Jordanian television (which we can get) so that she can finally see him and try and send an offer of marriage to him – now that would make a hell of a story! No novelist has come up with that one yet: *a young Israeli girl soldier at a listening post falls in love with a Jordanian pilot from the sound of his deep voice. She risks her life to cross the border and be with him. Bewitched by her (he's always loved redheads), he asks if she'll spend the rest of her life with him. The two lovebirds desert their respective armies and get married in a Buddhist monastery in India.*

'Hey, spy, are you still with us?'

I come to with a start: I'd gone way, way off into the sky.

'I got a few hours' leave after getting my corporal's stripes,' I murmur. 'I went to a French cultural centre and I watched a really good programme about the French Revolution.'

They all look at me as if I've started talking in Chinese.

'I thought we should start a revolution too.'

They seem to think I'm getting worse by the minute, but I carry on. I've suddenly got plenty to tell them.

'Hey, yes! Listen: what did we learn in school? That we live in a wonderful country which people built with their own hard work and by fighting against other states who wanted to see it die. The whole thing set to background music where the words "land", "fields", "streams" and "soldier" constituted eighty per cent of the lyrics. We were also told that it was now our turn to "give something to our country", to join the army and follow in the footsteps of the heroes who defended the State. All that's very well, but it's not the whole truth any more.'

'What is the truth?' Freddy asks, watching me intently.

'Well, we should stop dominating another people, we should withdraw from Judea, Samaria and Gaza. Then we could really get down to tackling the problems in this country. And we just can't go on accepting the fact that some people get a pittance of a salary while others have so many shares they don't know what to do with them. Wasn't this meant to be a socialist Jewish state? Well, let it really be one! We'll refuse to go on making students pay incredible registration fees when religious figures – who, I should remind you, don't do national service and only pay taxes about once every seven years – are given state subsidies to study –'

'And Jerusalem, what would you do with Jerusalem?' asks Yulia, always betraying me just at the crucial moment.

My heart feels heavy: I can't imagine the city cut in two. Feelings have nothing to do with politics, but all the same . . . Can one half of a body survive without the other?

'I don't know . . . we'd find some sort of intelligent solution.'

Yulia is triumphant, and she's not about to stop when she's doing so well.

'And what about socialism . . . do you think socialism made people happy in the Soviet Union?'

'That's not the same, that was a totalitarian state. Israel's a democracy, and I'm only asking for a little bit more equality for everyone,' I reply, sure of myself this time.

'But the Palestinians launch attacks every day, we can't hold discussions with them!' Ilana protests.

'It's not a question of knowing whether or not we *can*. We *have* to! For their sakes as much as our own.'

'What do you mean?' Rahel intervenes.

'If we stay in the territories, if Tsahal goes on training its weapons on a civilian population, the worst will happen: the world will no longer see us as admirable pioneers – we're not like that any more, anyway. But the worst of it would be we'd no longer dare to look at ourselves in the mirror. And more and more people will die . . . . for nothing. Look at Ilan: he doesn't even want to talk about what it's like over there. If the military action there was really glorious, you'd have come out and said something, wouldn't you?' I say, staring forcefully at him.

'That's not the point,' he says hesitantly. 'I think you're kidding yourself if you think peace is possible . . .'

'But peace isn't little birds singing and flowers growing all of a sudden, like in songs! I say we've got to sort out this conflict once and for all, and let this country be what it wanted to be when it was born: egalitarian, constructive, full of solidarity!'

'Shush . . . you're getting too loud,' Freddy warns me, but it's too late: I'm soaked from head to foot. The old Romanian woman who's just emptied a bucket of water over my head is a better shot than an elite marksman.

'Hmph! Midnight!' she grumbles as she closes her shutters. 'What sort of time is this to be talking politics! Not under my window, anyway!'

I resent her terribly, not because I'm streaming with water while the others try their best to stifle their laughter, but because I won't be able to see my reasoning through to the end and convince my friends.

'But revolutions are always planned at night!' I shout at the closed shutters.

Back at home, I run back over the text from New Zealand which Kineret read to us during our course.

I wouldn't like to live in a country where there's nothing to change.

Sunday morning, Beersheva central bus stop. There are two buses to Jerusalem (which I have to go through to get back to

192

the base): the 405, which goes round the territories and takes an hour and forty-five minutes to get there, and the 440 which passes the Judea desert, going through the Palestinian towns of Hebron and Bethlehem. In an hour and twenty-five minutes you're on the outskirts of the Holy City.

The bus which takes this route would be recognisable in a thousand: it's covered in dust and the windows are dotted with star shapes, caused by stones which have lent their name to the Palestinian uprising – the 'war of stones' or Intifada.

I get on to the 440 bus knowing that, this time, I won't go to sleep. I've been living in Israel for five years and, like most Israelis apart from soldiers posted there on military service, I've never set foot in the territories. It's high time I knew more about it than what you see on TV.

There are about 20km of desert-like country between Beersheva and the first Palestinian villages. It's silly, but I hadn't realised they were so close. I start seeing little stone houses, often on stilts, among the thorny bushes and the rutted tracks. An incredible proportion of them are unfinished. What's even more amazing is that most of them have been topped with antennae in the shape of . . . the Eiffel Tower! They strike me as grotesque and touching. So that's the real Palestinian dream: Paris!

'It's raining,' says someone on the bus. 'It's better when it rains, we don't get so many stones.'

From his beard and his kippa, I can tell he's a Jew who lives in the territories, what the pacifists call a 'colonist'. Does he check the weather forecast before taking the bus?

The villages are spread out over several kilometres. No one knows where one place ends and another begins. Poverty, sadness, hatred. I can see all that on the occasional faces that turn to look at the red and white bus. Old men leaning on walking sticks – they look noble somehow, like the beautiful Bedouins in *Lawrence of Arabia*. Children in ill-fitting clothes. Women with heavy figures and tired faces, balancing baskets on their heads. There are some girls in grey uniform coming out of a school and shouting at us – something I'd rather not hear. Ageless Mercedes, donkeys, herds of sheep, olive trees.

I feel like I've crossed a border, but not a geographical one. Where am I? A hundred, two hundred years back?

The towers of the minarets catch your eye. Every now and then, on a hill, you can see the red tiles of a Jewish settlement.

The bus makes frequent stops, dropping off soldiers going back to their camps and civilians going home. There are only about ten of us left as we approach Hebron, the largest town in Judea. All the passengers have wisely chosen to sit along the aisle. Except for me. I've got my nose pressed up against the window. I want to see everything.

A violent thudding sound, right beneath my face. I just had time to see a teenage boy twirling his sling. His face was hard and vengeful. He was aiming for me, I'm sure of it. I'm wearing army uniform, I'm the supreme enemy.

I feel like opening the window and shouting at him, 'Hey! I'm the same age as you and I think just what you think!'

But the stones are hailing down on us at the moment. The

driver accelerates, going over the legal speed limit, but I'd be surprised if he were stopped for that: the only form of authority in the territories is the Israeli army.

Everyone in the bus is on the floor, including me. We're thrown from right to left and from left to right to avoid projectiles. The impact of each stone inflicts pain on me as if I'm being hit. I hear an explosion. I can't tell who fired, whether anyone's been killed or wounded. I burst into tears and the other passengers try to reassure me. I don't feel like explaining that I'm not crying because I'm frightened.

SOLDIER GIRLS CRY TOO

I managed to get hold of Jean-David on the phone yesterday. I told him I had leave for the night and I felt like sleeping somewhere other than the base.

He hesitated for a bit, then he said, 'You can come, but I've got friends coming over this evening.'

I had a horrible feeling of foreboding, but I fought it back, telling myself I had to see him, that my need was stronger than me, stronger than my fear of rejection.

'I'll leave the keys for you at the cleaners opposite,' he added. 'I'll be there at about seven.'

It felt good going into his house on my own, as if we lived together. I had a shower, put my own clothes on and snuggled under his duvet with a book I'd borrowed from the Alliance Française.

I didn't read a single line.

I was in his bed, wrapped in the smell of him which I inhaled deeply, with my eyes closed. Then I opened them and I saw it.

A make-up bag.

A bottle of perfume, Giorgio of Beverly Hills, which I sniffed knowing it was a smell I'd loathed all of my life.

A Kookaï T-shirt.

A girl's deodorant.

I started to shake and I begin to talk out loud, saying over and over again, 'It's his cousin, it's his cousin, she must have come over from France to see him.'

He never told me he had a cousin.

Just then I heard a key in the lock and I pulled the duvet right up to my chin, pretending to be asleep. At least he'd have to be gentle with me just for a few seconds, to wake me up.

He stroked my hair with a sad hand.

I opened my eyes and looked over towards the make-up bag. He didn't say 'My cousin's come to stay', he sighed.

I shoved my book into my bag and headed for the door. He tried to hold me back.

'At least stay and have supper with us!'

I burst out laughing, a hopeless, despairing laugh.

'I don't want you to be hurt,' he said in a stubborn voice.

'Well, you've failed,' I replied and slammed the door.

I just had time to see a girl a bit older than myself (22 or 23) looking at me in astonishment. She wasn't even pretty.

In the bus on the way back to the base, I sobbed like I never have before, not even when he left me the first time.

The woman sitting next to me was worried and asked where it hurt, then whether someone had died. I didn't manage to give her an answer, so she hugged me to her and cradled me for the whole journey, and she kept saying that everything would be fine, everything would be fine and that there was a God for those who suffered. I would never have imagined finding refuge beside a complete stranger whose face I didn't even see and whose name I'll never know.

Back at the base I looked for the girls who were on guard duty that night. Heidi from ten till two in the morning. Noa from two till six. I offered to take their place. They didn't say anything about my red eyes, they just floated the idea that it might not be within the regulations to do two guard duties in a row. I told them that was my business. They didn't insist, too grateful to be able to sleep without interruption.

I patrolled the base with Ofer, a milouimnik* who told me about his travels in India. He told me that he'd set off the first time because his girlfriend had left him.

'I felt like I'd turned into a block of ice and I needed to warm myself up under different skies.'

At about four o'clock in the morning, the muezzin in the neighbouring village called the faithful to prayer.

'They're insulting us,' Ofer told me (he understands Arabic perfectly). 'And they're promising us we'll be in hell soon.'

My teeth were chattering with the cold and exhaustion,

---

* A soldier in the reserves, i.e. any man aged between 22 and 25 who does one month of (paid) military service a year.

but I found the strength to reply.

'Tell him not to bust a gut. In my case, the work's all done, I'm there already.'

He looked at me kindly.

'I can't stand the sound of that muezzin,' he said. 'You couldn't sing a French song, could you, so that we can't hear him any more?'

In a shaky voice I started on the chorus of that song Jean-David used to like: 'Tell me, tell me then, that she left for someone else but me . . .'

We sang quietly together for two hours, in Hebrew and in French, songs by Edith Piaf and many others, some of which I was surprised to discover he knew by heart when I hardly knew them.

I'm on duty in half an hour. I haven't slept for twenty-four hours. I'm exhausted. That's exactly what I wanted.

In a few days it'll be the 1st of April. I'll be nineteen, and I'll be on holiday. About every six months we're entitled to a 'long' leave of a week. I've made loads of plans but I know I'll spend at least half the time doing what all soldiers do on leave: sleeping.

In the meantime, we're all in the TV room at the base, gathered round Eynat the redhead who's bubbling with excitement. The Jordanian pilots' course finishes today, and she's finally going to be able to see her Prince Charming's face.

In order to be sure we can identify our man, we've requisitioned an officer from another section who knows the real names of the men we recognise by their code names. I think he's smiling in a peculiar way.

The ceremony begins, in the presence of King Hussein and Queen Noor. Military parade, display of combat exercises, all the guests pretending to be very interested by the show when they're actually profoundly bored . . . unlike us, drinking in the images as if it's a video of Papuan Indians we've suddenly discovered we're related to.

The big moment's coming. *Eagle One*'s going to give the silver wings to each of the trainee pilots – the same ones he's been insulting mercilessly for eighteen months. A white dot moves towards the platform where the pilots are standing to attention.

'Close up! Close up!' we bellow at the TV.

'His real name's Adnan B.,' our officer friend informs us, his smile becoming more obviously ironic by the minute.

'I think that means "delicate" in Arabic,' Noa tells Eynat who's holding her breath.

'Close up! Close up! Close up!' the others are still chanting.

Suddenly the Jordanian camera man does something he should never have done: he grants our wish and zooms in on *Eagle One*, alias Adnan B.

Adnan B., major and instructor.

Adnan B. with the warm deep voice.

Adnan B. whose personal quirk is singing Beatles songs at the end of each exercise, his favourite being *Yellow Submarine*.

Adnan B. who Eynat genuinely seems to be in love with (however improbable that may seem).

Adnan B., alias *Eagle One*, 1m55, bald, tubby, with a moustache and well over fifty.

An awkward silence reigns on the Israeli front at the moment, while the Jordanians release clouds of multi-coloured balloons to the sound of a fanfare. Never has the rift between the two states been so deep, I would say.

No one dares look at Eynat, who's prostrate in her chair.

'But that can't be him,' Emek whispers to our officer spy.

He nods his head with affected regret. Now I understand his little smile earlier on.

'You're cruel,' I tell him, to make sure he knows I wasn't taken in.

'No, I'm not,' he replies coolly. 'It's not what someone looks like that matters, is it? At least that's what girls never stop saying. According to our sources, Adnan has a superior intellect, is extremely cultured, considerate, sensitive and . . . a widower. What more could you ask for?'

A hand lands swiftly on his left cheek. Eynat's hurled herself at him in a fury, and we have a lot of trouble holding her back. On top of her disappointment, we really can't have her spending a few weeks in prison for slapping an officer!

The injured party rubs his cheek thoughtfully and murmurs, 'We'll consider this incident to have taken place outside the military context. I won't lodge a complaint. Goodnight and . . . my commiserations, young lady.'

I'm surprised by his reaction – or rather his lack of reaction – to Eynat's attack. There are only two possible explanations: he's an extraterrestrial or he's actually British. A third possibility: he's barely twenty years old, after all, and, like most Israeli lieutenants, he just wanted to have a bit of fun.

For the first couple of days of my leave I feel completely disorientated: it feels like a whole ocean of time. I sleep till midday, have lunch late in the afternoon, lie in my bath for hours and devour three books in two days. I haven't been out of uniform for more than 48 hours for seven months. I can even almost forget that I'm a corporal in the Israeli army. I'm free to go to the cinema with Yulia, and it's my birthday tomorrow and we're going clubbing in Tel Aviv with Freddy.

We stop in a bar to drink a bit and talk a lot. I realise that I'm having trouble accepting Yulia as she is now (too sure of herself, too seductive and abrasive), but she's the one I can really laugh hysterically with. She's irresistible, especially when – like today – she imitates our old schoolteachers, her base commandant, the Prime Minister or Paint-pot. The nastiness in her which sometimes bothers me turns into fierce humour.

It's three in the morning when we finally get home, arm in arm, moderately plastered on vodka cocktails.

'Hey, there's a light on in your house,' she tells me, looking up at the first floor of 12, Safed Street.

Mum's awake, but that doesn't surprise me: in fifty years' time she'll still be ringing me at home in the evenings to check that I've got back all right, and only then will she go to bed, reassured at last.

But the concern I can see in her sleepy eyes doesn't have the same taste as usual.

She speaks very seriously, telling me that Major Ouri has rung to say my leave has been suspended, without explaining why, of course. I'm expected back at the base at nine o'clock at the latest. I've got three hours to pack my bag, sleep and sober up.

OPERATION BLUE POPPY

I 'celebrate' my nineteenth birthday in the bus taking me back to the base, dog tired but woken with a start every now and then by one question: why've I been called back right in the middle of my leave? If a war had broken out, I'd already know about it.

But maybe a war's about to break out and they need the listening service at full strength to fend off the worst of it.

8.57 a.m. I put my bag down on my bed, run to the bunker, brandish my badge under the nose of the duty officer by the double security doors and push with all my strength to open the armoured door to the 'Printing Press'.

I instantly understand what's meant by the expression 'a highly charged atmosphere'.

The listening room is heaving with people. Every soldier in

the section is there, some of them with two sets of head-phones on. All the tape machines are running, there are ten people on the main platform, and everyone's shouting, warn-ing, giving snappy orders and calling out code names I don't recognise.

Ouri, who's just noticed that I'm here, rushes over and explains quickly, 'They're changing all the frequencies and all the code names. Quick, come and take over from Yariv doing the sweep!'

I sit down on the little platform in front of the computer sweeping the frequencies. This operation, called 'Spring-Clean', was meant to be happening next week: all the infor-mation we have names the date as the 8th of April. The Jordanians are proving to us that they're keen practical jokers: it's the 1st of April.

There are several numbers flashing simultaneously on my screen. I stay on each frequency for ten seconds and, as I go along, I transmit the information to Ouri and to the soldier taking over on the tape machine. It goes something like this:

'Frequency 176, a squadron of three planes!'

'245, control tower!'

'189, radar station!'

'165, some clicking!'

'213, two planes, *Goal One* and *Goal Two*!'

'310, a pilot and a co-pilot!'

'278, they're talking in Arabic!'

'213, a squadron, I don't know how many planes!'

'213, correction, three planes, *Camel One, Two, Three*!'

At about 3 p.m. the fever pitch drops. I haven't seen the

time go by. The excitement and the speed of it all have given me wings. We're all smiling from ear to ear, happy that we've coped with the situation. And it's now that the other work begins: listening back through all the tapes, slicing up the information, putting everything in the right order – the code names, frequencies, squadrons and control towers; recognising the voices one by one to work out that *Hunter One* has become *Tiger One*, and that the airbase codenamed *Desert* is now called *Holyland*.

At 11 p.m. we stop this teeming, meticulous work, on our knees. Just two soldiers stay on in the listening station – all activity is as good as suspended at this time of day, except when there are night exercises. But there's no chance of that sort of thing happening tonight, I'm sure the Jordanians are as exhausted as we are. I take over from Noa, hooked up to the line from the international airport at Amman. A French plane is coming into Jordanian airspace.

'*Air France 847, flying from Paris to Baghdad, good evening, Amman!*'

'*Good evening, Air France 847, what is your height?*'

'*Five thousand feet.*'

'*OK, five thousand feet.*'

'*AF 847 to Amman, it's my co-pilot's birthday today. Do you want to say something to him?*'

'*Of course, avec plaisir!*' he says in French.

I almost pass out when I hear the Jordanian air-traffic controller intoning 'Happy birthday!' in French. The French pilots burst out laughing and thank their impromptu birthday singer. And I smile to myself, thinking at least someone's celebrated my birthday with me. And it doesn't really matter that he has absolutely no idea.

It takes us several days to decipher all the tapes on the operation which the Jordanians rather prettily called 'Blue Poppy'. My leave has been postponed indefinitely . . . I'm not happy about that, but what choice do I have?

As a consolation, I've been given mini-leave for a weekend. I'm free from four o'clock on Friday afternoon till six o'clock on Saturday evening. That's exactly the duration of the Sabbath, the Jewish day of rest, and the buses don't run that day. Of course, I've got used to hitchhiking (which I really like: there's something very exciting about this game of chance on the roads where you spend time with complete strangers who pour out their life stories and who I sometimes confide in, knowing I'm very unlikely ever to meet them again), but Beersheva is too far from Jerusalem, and I can't run the risk of getting back to the base late on Saturday evening.

(If . . . if Jean-David still loved me, I could have . . . we could have . . . Shush! The speculation hurts.)

What should I do? It would be too stupid to stay at the base. That would be like winning a fortune on the lottery and not changing anything about your life, or like having a free flight to Venice and not going because you don't want to spend money on the taxi to the airport.

Tel Aviv is only 60km from Jerusalem. If I get my skates on, I'll just get the last bus at five o'clock. For the return trip, I know my chances of getting a lift back to Jerusalem are better in a really big seaside town than in a small town in the middle of the desert.

The number 400 bus is setting off just as I arrive at the bus station. I run after it waving my arms and shouting, 'Wait! Wait!' I know I look completely ridiculous, but I've made up my mind I'm going to see the sea, and nothing's going to get in my way. The driver must have seen me in his rear-view mirror. He slows down, slides open the door and smiles at me kindly.

'Slow down, soldier girl, take your time. Do you think I wouldn't wait for a soldier going home?'

I thank him and sit down on the floor in the middle of the aisle. At this time of day there are no seats left. But, for months now, I've been able to sit pretty much anywhere and to sleep pretty much anywhere. The main thing is just being on the bus that's taking me where I want to go.

The Soldiers' Hostel (a sort of youth hostel reserved for soldiers – quite right too!) isn't far from the beach. I take a room which probably hasn't been redecorated for thirty years and set off into the streets of Tel Aviv.

And there's the sea, in front of me, edged with luxury hotels where three corporals' wages would hardly be enough to pay for a room looking out over the garages and the kitchens.

I feel euphoric. Like the day when I faked an accident with my glasses to get off the base during an exercise. I've got this delicious feeling I'm playing truant, that I'm even freer because I'm anonymous here and because no one who knows me knows where I am. I didn't ring home to tell them about my leave. They might have been upset that I hadn't done everything I could to spend a few hours at home or with my friends.

I've taken my sandals off, and my feet are sinking into the sand warmed by the burning sun which you can get here in April. I bite my lip: I didn't think to ask whether the Soldiers' Hostel has an armoury. I obviously can't swim with my Uzi submachine gun, unless I'm determined to get the thing rusty. And I definitely can't leave it on the beach, even if I politely ask someone to keep an eye on my weapon for five minutes, just while I take a dip.

So, no bathing today.

Shame, triple shame. I'm never more relaxed than when I'm in the water. It's the same for everyone, actually. I don't know anyone who could have a flaming row while they're swimming, or who's ever sobbed underwater, or who's felt waves of loathing for mankind while floating on their backs.

Conclusion: Franco, Hitler and Mussolini didn't do much floating.

It's with this thought in mind that I roll my combat trousers up to my knees and, with my gun slung across me, I walk along the beach as if I'm on guard duty. Only my toes and ankles will get a taste of salt water today.

Mind you, some people seem to be enjoying the show. A group of Dutch tourists are whooping enthusiastically at the sight of me: Clic! Clic! Great picture! I can already see them showing the picture off in Amsterdam or wherever, saying, 'In Israel there are soldiers everywhere. And girl soldiers too.

Some of them patrol the beaches and make the most of the opportunity to go for a paddle.'

That's how myths evolve. Actually, if they thought a bit, they'd realise that I'm nothing like as tanned as them, given that I spend my days in a bunker that never sees the sun and where the temperature's about 15°C, the ideal ambient temperature for the listening equipment.

But the delighted Dutchmen aren't satisfied with a long shot. They want to chat, to have their pictures taken with me, to take a typical local memory home with them. (And maybe they'd like to buy my cap, my insignia, my uniform, my identity tag and my weapon while they're at it.)

'You've got this a bit wrong. I'm not Donald Duck, and this isn't Disneyland,' I tell them, keeping my dignity.

I speak in French but they don't understand that any more than Hebrew, and that's hardly surprising really. So I explain in English that the army forbids the photographing of soldiers without special permission (which is half true) and that I'm very sorry, but that's just the way it is.

This time they're not whooping but wailing with disappointment and I leave them to it, with a glance full of polite regret. I'm sure the Dutch are charming once you get to know them . . . but why is it that anyone labelled a 'tourist' is always more inane than average?

'You're too hard,' I tell myself. 'If you keep thinking like that you'll turn into a bitter and intolerant old maid.' So, terrified of what's in store, I decide not to be so negative and to smile at the person next to me.

The person next to me happens, in this instance, to be a

boy of about twenty (in civilian clothes) who takes my smile as some sort of invitation and suggests very discreetly that I should share his bed tonight. I pretend I'm deaf. He sniggers, reckoning (quite rightly) that Tsahal doesn't enlist people with that sort of handicap. I leave the beach (there are definitely too many people on it), promising myself I'll get up at dawn tomorrow to come back.

Destination the Soldiers' Hostel and my room with the flickering light. I suddenly feel like having a little break in my solitude. Gali lives in Tel Aviv – he's an old school friend with the most beautiful blue eyes on the planet, the most perfectly etched mouth I've ever seen and thick wavy brown hair. When he pitched up in the year before our *bac* a fierce rivalry developed between all the girls. The competition started up instantly without ever producing any sort of result. This gorgeous boy was sociable but he kept his distance. I quickly relegated my own chances: we weren't in the same class and when he met me in the corridor he didn't exactly look like he was thrilled to the core.

In the *bac* year we ended up in maths together. When it was raining in break once I took out a French translation of a book by Amos Oz, a major Israeli writer. Gali leapt over with a feverish gleam in his eyes and started talking passionately about France and French writers. He'd already read all the stuff I hadn't read (Gide, Proust, Sartre), and he talked to me as if I could somehow bring him closer to them. We sat outside the school for two hours that day, talking about God – who probably didn't exist but about whom so much had been written. Other impassioned conversations followed. I'd never had such an exchange of ideas with someone my age, or anyone in fact.

One day he invited me to drop in at his house on the way to Extrapharm. I loved his room: a mattress on the floor (I felt, and still do, that's there's nothing more middle class than sleeping in a bed), books on every possible surface, a few candles, fishing nets hanging from the ceiling and on the walls.

Without knowing why, I was shaking.

Lighting a cigarette from the one that he'd just finished, he offered to read me some passages from the diary he was holding. It was really beautiful, mostly sad and violent thoughts on happiness, God and love. I shook more and more. I felt like he was laying himself bare to me. He carried on reading and his voice was just a whisper when he said, '. . . because I, Gali, am a homosexual.'

I was bowled over by the fact that he'd confided in me, it felt like a huge demonstration of trust. By the end of the year we were really close, even though we didn't see each other very often. He wasn't keen to mix with my friends. While we were taking the *bac* he told me his parents were moving to Tel Aviv. He was glad to be leaving this chin-wagging, provincial little town for somewhere where he could be himself without anyone making fun of him.

Since then he's written me two or three beautiful letters, and I've been quite slow to write back, thanks to a succession of exciting new films (*The Break-up, The Course, The Break-down, The Break-up 2, Operation Blue Poppy* . . .). He said I could go and see him whenever I liked.

I dialled his number and when he answered he was clearly pleased to hear from me. When I told him I was in Tel Aviv he said we should meet up.

'Tonight at about ten, at the Picasso Café, facing the sea, not far from the French embassy.'

I'm a bit nervous about seeing him again. It's almost a year since we took the *bac*, and so much has happened since then.

He's walking towards me. His eyes are still as blue, his hair is shorter (with military service it can't be helped) and there's a little smile on his lips. We hug and pick up our conversation as if it had stopped the day before. He's not surprised by my long silences, he understands everything even before I've finished each sentence. He's happy to offer his friendship without asking for anything in return.

I'm not used to that sort of relationship: with my girl-friends it's more affection, passion, possessiveness, jealousy – the whole nine yards. With him, there's a gentle dialogue between us, and I can't see how I've got by without him for so long. I talk to him about the writer Stefan Zweig, he talks to me about Thomas Mann. He talks Verdi to me, I talk Brahms to him. I tell him about the still unhealed wound of missing Jean-David, he tells me about his boyfriend who regularly plays 'I won't call you and we'll soon see who gives in first'.

I tell him about my mini-breakdown during my course and the suffocating feeling I often get when I want to get out of the base but I can't. He nods and says he wouldn't have been able to put up with what I've had to put with. After a short course he managed to get himself transferred to the army's cultural department. He goes down to be by the sea every evening.

We also talk about the political situation. He says we'll have to give everything back, give it all to the Palestinians, including the bit of Jerusalem they want from us. He thinks that there's no price on life, and that's the only worthwhile slogan.

'Tel Aviv never sleeps, but I think you do,' he says at about four in the morning.

My eyelids do seem to be very heavy. But if I go to sleep now I won't keep the promise I made to myself: to go back to the sea at dawn. I suggest that we go and sit down by the water and wait for the first rays of light together. We sit in gentle silence watching day break over Tel Aviv, dipping our feet in the water.

WHEN AN OLD MAN DIES
IT IS LIKE A LIBRARY BURNING
(AFRICAN PROVERB)

19th September, 3.30 p.m.

*I don't know whether I should write 'one year gone already'
or 'one year to go'. I'm exactly halfway through, but that
doesn't make it seem any shorter. Mind you, we are gaining
one advantage with passing time: along with the other girls
on the course, I'm beginning to look almost like an old
hand. New soldiers have joined the ranks of this section,
they're a few months younger than us, but that's enough to
land them with the worst chores and guard duties. I've
grown fond of the hills and stones around the base. This
place has become my home.*

I'm taking the bus to Tel Aviv today. Since April when I met
up with Gali again, I've become a regular passenger on the
400 bus. As soon as I have a day's leave, I sneak off to this
unique city: most of it is incredibly ugly, 1930s houses have

been left to age and not been granted even a dab of make-up, and then right next to them there are tower blocks trying to be so modern, each more modern and high-tech than the last.

An ugly city, yes, but one that lives at full tilt, as if tomorrow never comes, as if everyone's going to die in a few hours so they have to dance one last time, have one last drink, intoxicate themselves with love, music and booze before going under.

Tel Aviv, the biggest city in Israel, and one which tries to forget it's in Israel, just a few kilometres from the Palestinian territories. Tel Aviv which believes in the sea, the cafes and the discos, like Jerusalem believes in God.

The two cities don't actually like each other and have been locked in a nameless war since 1926 when Tel Aviv was born (to the contempt of the 3,000-year-old Jerusalem). There's an old joke that goes: 'Name a place that someone from Tel Aviv likes better than Jerusalem. Answer: the road to Tel Aviv.' And vice versa.

I've completely fallen for both cities. I never tire of the stones of Jerusalem, of the light exploding over them, the smells and faces, and the religions – Jewish, Christian, Muslim – that have fashioned its streets. I like wandering through the Arab souk in the Old Town, drinking Turkish coffee (thick, bitter and served in a glass), or snacking on Arab bread flavoured with sesame or thyme. I watch the devout Jews beside the Western wall with fascination, this vestige of a temple ruined by the Romans 2,000 years ago which is mistakenly called the Wailing Wall: the people who pray here, rocking back and forth, aren't wailing and lamenting. Their eyes are enraptured as if they can see something or someone I can't (God?), someone they know intimately and can ask to intervene in this world that's gone mad.

There are a thousand ways to describe Jerusalem but only one way to love it, which is what I do: endlessly walking from the Arab quarter to the Jewish quarter, from the Armenian quarter to the Christian quarter, from the ramparts of the Old Town to the cafes in the new town.

But I also need Tel Aviv to breathe the same air as 20-year-olds who want the world to be like them: free, outrageous, flitting from happiness to sadness, from flippancy to seriousness, only to feel all the happier afterwards.

Gali and I have established our headquarters in Sheinkin Road, the only road in the world where there is one cafe for every inhabitant. We sit talking for hours at the Café Cazé, alongside writers finishing their books gazing deep into their cups of coffee. And anyone who isn't writing is dreaming of writing one day.

Like Gali, and like me.

Like Gali and like me everyone here thinks there needs to be a revolution, and we sometimes go and demonstrate with the 'women in black' calling for Israel's withdrawal from the Palestinian territories. They wear black as a sign of mourning and they're treated to torrents of abuse from the right-wing counter-demonstrators every Friday. (Last week I told Gali that it looked to me like the black of mourning was the representative colour for the left wing).

Sometimes we agree to drop politics from our conversation, to lock it away – it's exhausting wanting to change a world which stays obstinately the same. Then we turn to books: Gali tells me I really have to read Joyce's *Ulysses*, I tell him he really has to read Schnitzler's *Vienna by Twilight*. I like having a friend who, like me, thinks you can't run the risk of dying without having read certain books.

Some of his friends join us sometimes, people who've already left the army. They're aged about twenty-two to forty, and they're film makers, students, actors and painters by day . . . and waiters by night.

In Tel Aviv I forget that I'm a soldier.

Today Gali's decided to introduce me to his dearest friend, Zvi Kaminski. The first time he mentioned him to me he said, 'He's the oldest bookseller in Tel Aviv, he's seventy-five. No one in the world is better than him for cheering you up and making you laugh. He loves laughing at himself and being kind to other people.'

We go into this tiny little nook of a shop with books piled right up to the ceiling. There are a few people sitting on pouffes, sipping tea, clustered round a man with a beard and white hair. He reminds me of the carpenter Geppetto in *Pinocchio*. I feel intimidated, but as soon as he sees us, Zvi Kaminski gets up and gently tells the others to leave.

'Come on, we've dug over the past enough, make way for the youngsters. And anyway, at least this boy buys books from me!' he says affectionately, pointing at Gali. His eyes twinkle, I see what Gali meant. We sit down on the pouffes.

'Hello, Valérie.'

I flash a quick look of surprise at Gali.

'Well, of course he's told me about you, at least as much as he's told you about me!'

I don't know what to say. Right now, I'm blessing that illustrious somebody who invented good manners.

'I'm very pleased to meet you, Mr Kaminski.'

'Mr Kaminski! Last time I was called that was in Poland before the war! We shouldn't talk about depressing things like that, we should be getting to know each other instead: do you take your tea with sugar or without?'

'Yes, with, please.'

'Well, that's perfect then, you love life, but I already knew that. I'm going to get some clean glasses.'

While he's away, Gali whispers, 'He's offered you tea, so you're in! You could come back here any time, even in the middle of the night, and he'd open up the shop just for you.'

Zvi comes back whistling Schubert's *Unfinished Symphony*. I can't keep my eyes off the piles of books, and the craftsman who created this bizarre construction says brightly, 'You're a bit surprised by all this jumble, aren't you?'

'A bit, yes.'

'Well, that's what I'm trying to do, to surprise people when they walk in here. Books don't like being arranged in alphabetical order or by subject. Alphabetical order makes for some unfortunate pairings, and doing it by subject ends up being boring. A historical essay doesn't mind being put next to a novel about love . . . it gives it a chance to relax, to think about something else. I hate bookshops that look like chemists,' he says, pulling a face. 'Everything's organised, people come in with their little lists (the prescription), talk quietly (there are sick people around) and they pay quickly before scuttling off. It's so depressing!'

'But you do recommend reading like you were prescribing medicine,' Gali pipes up.

'Mmmm, you're not wrong there . . . but that's as it should be. You can't give Kafka's *The Trial* to someone whose relationship's just breaking up, they might never recover.'

'And what would you recommend to someone whose relationship's breaking up?' I ask, acutely interested.

He looks at me kindly.

'First I'd tell them to cry to their last tear, till they feel as dry as the soil of this country. Then to open *Belle du Seigneur* by Albert Cohen – he's a compatriot of yours. A thousand pages of love and of love breaking down, that's pretty radical.'

A little bell rings in my pocket, abruptly silencing Zvi Kaminski – I could die of shame. For a month now, every soldier in the section has had a beeper so that the base can get hold of us anywhere 24 hours a day. I scroll through the message.

URGENT: 3810159 return to base immediately. It's signed 3575028, that's our new commanding officer, Dvora.

I get up unwillingly and stammer that I have to go. Gali looks as heartbroken as I am; only Zvi is smiling.

'They're calling you back so that you'll be even more keen to get back here next time. This shop's been here for forty-three years and it's not about to close tomorrow. Here, take this for the road,' he adds, handing me a tiny book. I try to find my purse but Gali digs me with his elbow to mean: don't do that, he'll be offended. So I thank him as best I can, but it's not easy when you're touched as well as in a hurry.

In the bus on the way back (it was the same driver as on the way there, he didn't understand at all when he saw me), I opened the book Zvi had given me.

Poems on Jerusalem by Yehuda Amichai.

I buried myself in it straightaway.

Dvora's waiting for me at the gates of the base: a mass of curly red hair, big green eyes, quite a chubby face and an amazingly deep voice. She exudes an air of incredible efficiency. I get on much better with her than with our previous commanding officer: Ouri used to make pathetic jokes, whereas Dvora's actually got a sense of humour, which isn't the same at all. She sometimes works eighteen hours a day, and makes us feel like doing the same. She's turned nineteen and a half (in the army we're a bit like newborn babies, we calculate our age very precisely. A few months make a huge difference).

Dvora greets me with a wide smile, which is intended to reassure me, I imagine.

'Leave your things at the gate and come to my office,' she says.

She offers me some tea. I accept because I never finished the tea I was drinking in Tel Aviv. She picks up a pen and draws a little house as she talks to me.

'Right, a very special mission is going to be carried out tomorrow. Obviously, neither you nor I need to know what it's about. One of our planes is going to fly over the region with listening equipment on board. We've been asked to send someone, and I thought of you.'

My heart's beating fit to burst. Some of the older ones have already been on this sort of expedition. They came back very overexcited and kept this mysterious look on their faces for several days.

Dvora's still drawing, adding trees next to the house, a lake and a boat.

'You should know that there are risks involved,' she says, looking up. 'The plane won't stay in Israeli airspace, and it could be intercepted. You'll be protected, of course, but there's no such thing as zero risk.'

'Aren't you going to draw a plane?' I ask, pointing to the paper on her desk.

She winks and says, 'No, that's the house I'm going to have one day on Lake Tiberius*.'

I admire her for having precise plans – I only have dreams.

'Well?' she asks me.

'I'll come and visit you in your house,' I tell her, and then I add, 'And then I'll tell you how tomorrow's operation went.'

She gives a sigh of relief and her voice becomes even more serious when she says, 'Here are your orders for the mission. This evening you'll take the XXX bus to B. The base is one kilometre from there, indicated with a sign marked MK 1086. They'll explain everything there.'

She stands up and I do too. Then she shakes my hand.

---

* Another name for the Sea of Galilee.

'You'll see. When you've forgotten all about your military service, you'll remember this.'

And here I am in a bus again, the third of the day. If the Egged Company handed out loyalty cards, I'd be able to travel free for three centuries with the points I've accumulated. Night's falling very quickly; I'm ruining my eyes trying to make out the last verses of a poem by Amichaï.

I can feel a very kindly eye on me. To my right there's a very wrinkled, shrivelled old woman watching me infinitely tenderly.

'You remind me of someone,' she tells me, 'a good person.'

I smile back at her.

'So do you. You have my grandmother's eyes . . . and she was a very good person.'

I feel like we've said everything; what could you add after confiding in someone like that? But she goes on.

'You're a good girl and I'm sure you're a good soldier. I'd like to have had a daughter like you, but I didn't have any children. I was born in Vilna. Do you know where that is?'

My history lessons quickly resurface: Vilna, the capital of Lithuania, the new Jerusalem as it was known, the city of a thousand wise rabbis, before the Nazis got there. I nod my head, my stomach's in knots.

'The Germans came. They shot some of the Jews and herded the others into a ghetto. Why shoot one person and not another? I was twenty-two, I had a father, a mother, a younger brother and a younger sister. And a sweetheart, we were going to be married. He wanted to wait till the end of

the war, he said you can't have the best day of your life surrounded by death. His name was Yatsek.

'They killed my father on the first day. My mother fell ill
and she died soon afterwards. We were hungry, and cold. I
was frightened again, like when I was little and I was afraid
of the wolf at night. But now I was twenty-two and there
was a whole pack of wolves prowling round us day and night,
howling. Yatsek tried to run away from the ghetto and was
taken. No one ever saw him again.'

I'm crying silently. She goes on, with her hand on my arm.

'One day my sister and I went out to look for something to
eat. A German looked at us, burst out laughing, then pointed
his gun at me, at my sister, at me, at my sister, at me, at my
sister. In the end, she was the one he shot.

'Now there were just two of us. Shloimele, my younger
brother, and myself. We managed to escape from the ghetto
and we went into hiding with our old neighbours. We stayed
in their cellar for two years. At the end of the war they asked
if we would like to go on living with them, but we couldn't,
we had to leave that country which was gorged with the
blood of our people.

'In 1948, we set sail on a boat heading here. We arrived on
the first day of the war of independence. They took my
brother as he stepped off the boat, gave him a gun and told
him: "Go and fight with the others to defend your country."
He'd never held a gun. He was killed on the second day of
fighting.'

I don't even know if I'm still breathing. She finishes her
story calmly.

'Why did I live when they all died? There's no answer to that. You remind me of Yatsek's sister – that's why I've told you all this.' She pauses for a moment, then she adds, 'You mustn't cry, you mustn't cry. Now there are girls like you, with beautiful smiles, who can defend this country if need be. I never married, I didn't want to make someone unhappy all their life. But every child in this country is my child, and I feel so happy when I see you . . .'

I heave a very deep sigh. In a few minutes I'll have to get off, I have a mission to accomplish. A new blood is flowing in my veins, as if I were going to fight for this old woman with her gentle eyes, this woman whose hand shook as it held my arm.

TOP SECRET MISSION
AND A1 REUNION

An army air corps sergeant led me over to the tent.

'You'll sleep in here,' he told me. 'You'll be given some details tomorrow.'

Inside the tent there are six beds, three of which already seem to be occupied. The sergeant points out how to get to the showers and the refectory, and says he hopes I have a good night.

I'm no longer surprised by how bland some conversations can be in the army. What is quite fun, on the other hand, is sleeping in a different base. I don't know anyone, don't have any guard duties or chores to do, I almost feel like a tourist.

In the refectory I don't dare chat with the others. What am I allowed to tell them about why I'm here? On the other hand, I do appreciate the cook's talents, he seems to want to do less harm to the soldiers he's feeding than ours does.

I'm just finishing a fruit bun, thinking about

tomorrow,when I almost stop breathing: SOMEONE'S PUT BOTH THEIR HANDS OVER MY EYES! So, they have practical jokers in the air corps too, do they? I struggle, as a matter of form, and fall to the ground just as I hear a familiar voice whispering, 'So, IQ 625, have you deserted your unit and come to take refuge with us?'

Eynat! My friend from the first course, the friendliest madwoman I've ever met!

'But what are you doing here?' I ask her, amazed.

She pouts slightly.

'I should be asking you that, don't you think? You're in *my* base!'

'It hasn't got your name written on it,' I tell her, 'unless you're now called MK 1086.'

She sighs and casts her eyes to the heavens.

'Right, no messing about, give me an answer or I'll stick you on latrine duties straightaway. I've got some power here, you know.'

I stiffen and give her a perfect salute.

'At your service, corporal!'

She puts both her hands round my neck and pretends to strangle me. I nod at the intelligence service insignia on my shoulder and whisper, 'Can't breathe a word. Top secret.'

'Of course,' she exclaims, clicking her fingers, 'you're here for tomorrow. Well, my dear, we're in the same boat, or should I say on the same plane, you and me.'

Confused expression from me.

'Hey, you've forgotten I was posted to radars. Radars! Can

you see the connection with planes or do you want me to draw you a picture?'

I take her by the shoulders and shake her.

'Right, are we finally going to give each other a hug and celebrate this reunion, or are we going to spend all evening bitching at each other like two soldiers on a bus heading off for their first course?'

She takes me off to her room, slapping me on the back. She takes some biscuits and apple juice from a cupboard, it feels like playing tea parties.

She flops down on to her bed.

'Well?'

'You first,' I say, respecting the mistress of the premises.

'No, you first. What about your broken heart?'

'I did a remake.'

'What?'

'Yes, we vaguely saw each other again and then he very definitely dumped me a second time.'

'But you're mad! You should never go back to an ex! Never, never, never! If it didn't work the first time, why do think it would work the second?'

I can see that her argument makes perfect sense. And, more specifically, it didn't actually hurt talking about Jean-David.

She asks me more questions; it's a sort of friendly interrogation.

'What's the listening like?'

'Good, sometimes a bit routine, but there are lots of surprises too, like today.'

'And your friends in Beersheva?'

'We see each other less, of course. I think we still really like each other, or maybe it's our past together that we like. The three of us are heading in completely different directions. We don't dream the same dreams any more.'

'And the people in your unit?'

'Snobbish, patriotic, conscientious, but not nasty really. My commanding officer's a fantastic girl.'

I tell her about Gali too, and about Tel Aviv and Jerusalem. And then it's my turn to bombard her with questions.

She affects indifference as she says, 'Well, since we last saw each other . . . now where was that, then? Oh yes! In a base in front of the letters of fire, chanting "I swear!". Anyway, I've caught up since those prehistoric days.'

'Caught up?'

'Sexually speaking. I've been to three different bases: a course to be a radar operator, a first posting in the South, then another in the North. In each base I think I left someone with good memories . . .' she says with some satisfaction.

'But you didn't get involved, you didn't fall in love?' I ask her in amazement.

'No. It felt good at the time, that's all. I'll fall in love when I'm a grown up and when I'm quite sure I've got nothing more to learn about boys.'

'And right now?' I ask, gobsmacked by her cool.

'No one. I've only just arrived, but it won't take long . . .' she says with a wink, and adds, 'You know, I've often thought about you.'

'Me too. And, seeing as you've crossed my path again, I

solemnly swear I'm not letting go of you again till the end of your days. Or mine.' Then I add more seriously, 'What do you know about tomorrow?'

'Not much more than you, probably. There's going to be some action towards the East. Take your pick out of Jordan, Syria and Iraq. You know there's a lot going on in Iraq?'

'Yes, we've been given instructions to be especially vigilant if we tune in to pilots speaking Arabic – the Iraqis don't use English, unlike the Jordanians.'

'Tomorrow in the plane there'll be soldiers from the three main aerial spy services: the listeners, radar operators and photographers. There'll be loads of important officers who won't even bother to look at you. They have this way of mega-concentrating, it's pretty impressive.'

We dream for a while, side by side. She suddenly sits up with a start.

'It's already ten o'clock! We'll make your bed, because I have to be up early tomorrow. You're on holiday here, you haven't got much to do apart from going to the briefing at ten and the one at four in the afternoon. But I've got to work all day.'

I salute her again. We burst out laughing, each as happy as the other to be together again.

At ten o'clock there are about thirty of us gathered in a large classroom. A lieutenant colonel draws a sort of whale on the blackboard: it's the plane we'll be transported in. He shows each of us where we'll be, and indicates relay stations we'll be transmitting the information to. He also hands out a list of twenty or so code names that we haven't heard before: if we hear them we have to give the alert immediately (and to scarper, presumably).

I feel drunk: I'm really going to be right at the heart of an operation, with Eynat by my side. I can't settle to reading or writing. I wander about the base, singing and counting the hours. Take-off is scheduled for 10 p.m.

At four o'clock we have the second briefing and it comes as a huge disappointment. The lieutenant colonel tells us the operation has been postponed, the weather forecast is bad. But the sky overhead is blue . . . I console myself with the knowledge that I'll spend at least a day with Eynat.

The following day at 4 p.m. they confirm that the operation will go ahead. We have time to prepare ourselves. Eynat takes me up to her room and empties her wardrobe on to her bed.

'Are you doing your washing now?' I ask, thinking it's hardly the moment.

'Have you been up in a spy plane yet? No? Well, I'm sure you can imagine it's nothing like a Boeing flight from Paris to Tel Aviv. There are no comfortable seats, no hostesses handing out sweets, no carpet on the floor and the cabin's completely bare.'

'So?'

'So it's bloody freezing! You freeze in there, your teeth don't stop chattering. Every operation I've been on I've added another layer of clothes, and I still nearly die of the cold.'

'How many layers do you wear?'

'Four.'

I can't help but gaze admiringly at so much experience. Then I panic.

'But I haven't brought anything with me, apart from my anorak! No one told me!'

She points to a pile of sweaters and T-shirts:

'What about all that, did you think it was for the cook?'

As we head over towards the plane we look like big khaki-coloured Easter eggs. I've put on tights, three pairs of socks, a short-sleeved T-shirt, two long-sleeved T-shirts, two sweaters, my uniform and my anorak.

'I'm not getting very far with my *Spy Flying Above the Clouds* look,' I whisper to Eynat grumpily.

'Yeah, but as the *Spy Who Came in from the Cold* you're perfect!' she retorts gaily.

She hands me two bars of chocolate.

'Take it, for when you feel hungry. They usually make something for us to chew on but it's usually pretty dire. Clearly, just because we're risking our lives, that doesn't entitle us to better food.'

'You're like a mother and a grandmother to me, Eynat Haymovitch.'

Out by the plane, we're each given a large pack: a life jacket and a parachute. In the afternoon we were told how the parachute worked. I put up my hand to say that I'd never made a jump.

Someone joked, 'It doesn't matter. If you fall on enemy land, you'd be better off if your parachute didn't open.'

Everyone burst out laughing, but I shuddered.

And I'm shuddering again now, in the plane which has just taken off: with fear, excitement and cold (already).

There are thirty serious faces concentrating over their work. I've got my headphones on and I'm taking notes, the same notes I take at the base, but they mean something different at this altitude. Are we protecting ourselves from agents trying to infiltrate us? Is this a 'simple' airborne spy expedition? I got the feeling there were other planes taking off at the same time as us.

We stay in the air for two hours, with no notable incidents. When we land, the lieutenant colonel responsible for the operation says, 'You've worked well. Thank you, all of you.'

The next day, in the papers, there are articles about thousands of different things but not about that. And I go back to my base with a mysterious twinkle in my eye.

FREE

19th September, the following year, midday
Let's see which of us makes the other laugh the most. Eynat
and I are side by side in the same base where our military
lives started two years ago.

We're now twenty years old, and we're queuing up to go the
other way.

I was treated to a little party at the base yesterday but it
had to be brief because of rumblings in Iraq.

'We might be seeing each other again sooner than antici-
pated, girls,' said Dvora. 'If things get much worse, we'll be
needing reinforcements, and you'll be called up as reservists.'
But I don't want to think about that today. Eynat and I have
planned to party for twenty-four hours non-stop in Tel Aviv.
First we'll go for a swim, and she can meet Gali.

We hand back our uniforms, our anoraks, our jute kitbags,

and the shoes we haven't actually worn since those early lessons. We're allowed to keep our identity tags and our papers as souvenirs.

We're given a cheque for 200 shekels: a gift which goes with our freedom.

We look the jobniks up and down haughtily as they finish their menial tasks. Those who made fun of us two years earlier are no longer here, but that doesn't matter, we're getting our revenge.

As we leave the base, we give wild whoops of disbelief. We pass a bus full of young girls of eighteen in civilian clothes and with anxious expressions. We've come full circle.

On the beach we take our clothes off as quickly as we can. I point out to Eynat that we've got all the time in the world, we're not just on leave.

'You know,' I tell her, 'I really thought those two years were an eternity.'

She runs towards the sea, shouting, 'Well, we've got all eternity behind us, then!'

Valérie Zenatti

Valérie Zenatti was born in Nice, France, in 1970. When she was thirteen she moved with her family to Israel. It was there that she did the national service which inspired *When I Was a Soldier*. Even now she doesn't go anywhere without her survival kit—which these days includes a book, a notepad and a pen. She currently lives with her two children in Paris, where she works as a translator of Hebrew, and is continually surprised and delighted at seeing her children, Lucas and Nina, grow up. This is Valérie Zenatti's first book for Bloomsbury.